Never too old to Knit

Beautiful Basics for Baby Boomers

Never too old to Knit

Beautiful Basics for Baby Boomers

edited by Karin Strom

sixth&spring books

sixth&spring books
233 Spring Street
New York, New York, 10013

Editorial Director
Trisha Malcolm

Art Director
Chi Ling Moy

Graphic Designer
Sheena T. Paul

Book Division Manager
Erica Smith

Associate Editor
Erin Walsh

Yarn Editors
Tanis Gray
Veronica Manno

Instructions Editor
Pat Harste

Instructions Proofreader
Rita Greenfeder

Copy Editors
Kathy Edgar
Wendy R. Preston

Technical Illustrations
Uli Mönch

Fashion Photography
Dan Howell

Photo Research
Sue Ackerman

Photo Stylist
Christy Tagmeier

Production Manager
David Joinnides

President and Publisher, Sixth&Spring Books
Art Joinnides

Photo credits
Page 11 Fotosearch
Page 13: Index Stock Photos
Page 14: Aaron Flaum, TSS
Page 17: Tim Boyle, Getty Images
Pages 34, 50 and 76: Ronnie Kaufman, Corbis
Page 64: Jacqui Hurst, Corbis
Page 79: by Jose Luis Pelaez, Corbis

All instructional photographs feature Lion Cotton by Lion Brand Yarn in #123 Seaspray, #140 Rose, and #158 Banana.

1 3 5 7 9 10 8 6 4 2

Manufactured in China

Library of Congress Control Number: 2006925123
ISBN-10: 1-933027-08-8
ISBN-13: 978-1-933027-08-1

Table of Contents

Chapter one: Why knit?

Over the past several years, **KNITTING** has become more fashionable and exciting than ever — a generation- (and gender-) spanning **PHENOMENON**.

These days, needlecrafts make front-page news—a recent cover story in the *Wall Street Journal* examined the phenomenon of POWER KNITTING, and style maven Martha Stewart wore a handmade poncho as she made her famous jailhouse exit. If you're feeling left out because you don't yet know how to knit (or perhaps you've forgotten), join countless other women—AND men—in their prime who are finding out that there are other reasons to knit than competing with the young, hip, and famous. Yes, there's a lot more to knitting than celebrity watching. It's a way to add up-to-date FASHION ELEMENTS to your wardrobe and to bond with the younger generation. It's fun to do, and it's good for you, too! While knitting may not be the next fountain of youth, the experts agree—it does have HEALTH BENEFITS.

Granted, learning any new skill can seem daunting to the middle-aged mind (to say nothing of those aching hands), but knitting is really very simple. Just remember this: All knitting is made up of TWO BASIC STITCHES, the knit and the purl, and can be as easy or as complicated as you choose. (More on that later!) Meanwhile, in case you need convincing, whether you're a brand-new knitter or returning to the flock, here is something to consider:

The Top Ten Reasons to Start Knitting Now

1. Knitting Can Relieve Stress

Stress levels often seem elevated at midlife. Raging hormones tend to magnify every little problem. Working with the beautiful colors and textures of yarn can be very comforting, and the hand movements involved in knitting have a calming effect. Dr. Christiane Northrup, menopause guru and author of *The Wisdom of Menopause* (Bantam, 2001) concurs. "The repetitive hand motions of knitting are very soothing for the mind and emotions. It's the same concept we see with "worry" beads—and biting one's nails. These movements actually act like anxiolytics in the brain. But with knitting, as opposed to biting one's nails, you create beauty and order—instead of ragged cuticles!" In fact, according to Dr. Mona Lisa Schultz, author of *The New Feminine Brain* (Free Press, 2005), knitting has a similar relaxing effect on the brain as the anti-anxiety drug Valium. WARNING: Knitting May Be Addictive!

2. Knitting Is the New Yoga

Knitting has been dubbed the new yoga. But don't cancel your membership at the yoga studio just yet—the two go hand in hand. The Kripalu Center for Yoga & Health in Lenox, Massachusetts, offers classes combining knitting and yoga taught by longtime knitter and yoga practitioner, Karen Allen, who feels that the two practices perfectly complement each other. Medical studies prove her right. "Like meditation or prayer, knitting allows for the passive release of stray thoughts," says Dr. Herbert Benson of Harvard Medical School and author of *The Relaxation Response* (William Morrow, 1975). "The rhythmic and repetitive quality of the stitching, along with the sound of needles clicking, resembles a calming mantra," Dr. Benson explains. "The mind can wander while still focusing on one task." And if your shoulders get tight from too much knitting, try a Downward-Facing Dog.

3. Knitting Provides Mental and Creative Stimulation

Feeling a little fuzzy? As we age, blood begins to run at a slower rate to the brain, and using the brain less can result in a decrease in mental agility and flexibility. So grab some yarn, fuzzy or not, and a pair of needles to clear the cobwebs away. Recent research suggests that a brain workout on a regular basis can greatly reduce the risk of developing dementia. In the same way that crossword puzzles and chess stimulate the mind, knitting can keep the mental muscle in shape. Besides, working with the rainbow colors and sensual textures of yarns gets your creative juices flowing. Just walking into a great yarn shop can create sensory overload! There's no need to be overwhelmed, though—luckily, yarn shop owners are some of the most helpful folks on the planet!

4. Knitting Is Good for Your Health

The therapeutic benefits of knitting have long been put into use. During World War I, hospitalized soldiers learned to knit as a way to keep their minds off painful injuries. Knitting involves just the right combination of simple repetitive hand motion and mental focus to make it useful in a variety of rehabilitation situations from strokes to head injuries, according to Robin Hedeman of the Kessler Institute of Rehabilitation in New Jersey. It's used as an aid to smoking cessation and even weight loss. "It might seem ironic since knitting is a sedentary activity but working on a knitting project can help take the focus off food," states addictions counselor Karen Mell. Balance the sedentary side of knitting with frequent stretch breaks and walks to the yarn store.

And don't use your arthritis as an excuse not to knit! Like many knitters, you may find that the repetitive hand movements involved in knitting actually keep your joints lubricated. Try using wooden or bamboo needles and take frequent stretching breaks. Please check with your doctor before starting if your condition is severe.

5. Knitting Is Portable, Productive, and Oh So Glamorous

OK, you're probably getting tired of hearing about which svelte young actress has been spotted knitting this week. Perhaps the image of movie stars knitting on the sets of Hollywood productions seems a long way from the ancient pastime of shepherds who knit while watching their flocks, or sailors whiling away the endless hours aboard ships knitting caps, but you get the concept. Knitting is a great way to occupy your downtime. It's the perfect antidote for those of us who feel a certain touch of guilt just watching TV or just waiting for a plane or train. The very act of knitting seems to shorten those endless waits in doctors' offices.

Note for frequent flyers: The government's Transportation Security Administration includes knitting needles and crochet hooks on its official list of approved items for both carry-on and checked luggage for domestic travel. If you're traveling abroad, check with your airline to see if there are restrictions in the country you're visiting. If they don't allow knitting needles as carry-on, stash your project in your checked luggage. On-plane knitting etiquette tip: use shorter wooden or bamboo needles—and no elbowing your seatmate!

6. Knitting Is Ageless, Timeless, and Unisex

Marge Westcott, a 51-year-old Brooklyn, New York resident, recently asked her niece to teach her how to knit. Her niece, Sarah Westcott, 30, a location scout and avid knitter, learned knitting from her grandmother on the other side of the family, who in turn had learned from her mother. "I know it seems like the traditional roles are reversed, but I never took the time to learn when I was younger," Wescott explains. "I kept noticing all the terrific projects Sarah was knitting and finally I just couldn't wait!" Now they spend Saturday afternoons visiting the many wonderful yarn shops New York City has to offer. Judith L. Swartz, author of *Hip to Knit* (Interweave Press, 2002), has also observed this trend: "Lately I've noticed more girls teaching their grandmothers to knit, or at least giving them a refresher course, than the other way around!" Whoever teaches you (and we hope it's this book!), chances are you'll soon have a chance to pass it on.

Historians disagree about the exact beginnings of the craft of knitting, but whether it began in ancient Egypt or medieval Europe, one thing is clear—knitting is here to stay! Although many think of knitting as women's work, throughout history men have often been the star knitters. So, gentlemen, why not join shepherds, sailors, and soldiers of the past and jump on the knitting bandwagon? Be a part of today's resurgence of knitting among both sexes and keep tradition alive.

7. Knitting Provides an Opportunity to Give Back to the Community

A quick web search found almost one hundred organizations that distribute hand-knitted items to folks in need. Afghans for Afghans sends handmade blankets to displaced Afghani families, and Warm Up America creates cozy afghans one square at a time. Check out resources in your local community. Within your own community, places of worship, hospitals, and civic clubs often have programs organized to distribute layette items to premature babies, warm clothing to homeless families, and knitted toys to children in need.

8. Knitting Improves Your Wardrobe and Provides Countless Gift Giving Ideas

Is it an urge to augment your own wardrobe with fabulous knitwear, or maybe it's a new grandchild? Whatever inspires you to pick up the needles, most new knitters start with a frenzy of scarf making and graduate to more advanced projects such as hats, afghans, and sweaters. Yarn shop owners all over agree that one of the biggest motivations to learn knitting is the longing to make gifts. "Especially in the over-50 age group, from baby items for grandkids to hats for husbands and gifts for friends, the desire to make and give burns strong," says yarn shop owner Kathy Zimmerman of Kathy's Kreations in Ligonier, Pennsylvania. And let's not forget, knits are forgiving— they stretch—so they're flattering to figures of all ages!

9. Knitting Can Be Good for Your Social Life

Feeling a bit of empty nest syndrome or adjusting to the ironic stress of retiring? Your newfound hobby can help you meet new friends of all ages and discover a sense of community. Check out the library, community college, and yarn shops for classes and knitting clubs. Or consider joining a knitting guild through The Knitting Guild Association and be connected to a nationwide network of knitting groups. The group's website, www.tkga.com, provides a search by zip code to help you find a guild near you. You'll have instant access to its newsletter, educational programs, and conventions.

10. Knitting Promotes Shopping and Travel Opportunities

It's not just the fabulous yarn shops you'll be visiting on a regular basis (a recent Craftrends Magazine survey found that 64% of all yarn purchases in the United States are made by folks over 45). Think of the tote bags you'll need for all your knitting projects and the baskets to store the yarn. Oh, and

then you'll have to get a few pairs of those very hip magnifying glasses so you can see what you're knitting (the distinguished-looking half-glasses are perfect for knitting while watching TV). And, you might just decide to purchase a stylish new easy chair for your knitting comfort.

Finally, in case you still need convincing, consider that most places you visit virtually anywhere in the world have a textile tradition. You'll have a new reason to broaden your horizons—research! See Chapter 6: The Knitting Community for information on knitting camps, retreats, and foreign tours with knit-centric themes. And, remember, yarn is highly packable—so be sure to purchase souvenir skeins wherever you go!

Chapter two: Getting started

Now that you know the benefits of learning to knit,

it's time for all baby boomers to join the

KNITTING BOOM!

Before you get started, you'll want to do a little "market research." Visit your local YARN SHOP or the yarn section of a craft store to get a feel for what's out there and to start gathering some supplies. Spend some time searching the Internet checking for knitting-oriented WEBSITES. These days you can truly shop for just about anything without leaving your desk, but most knitters can't resist the visual, tactile, and SOCIAL PLEASURES of the yarn shop experience. When you visit your local yarn shop, introduce yourself as a new knitter. You'll be thrilled at the enthusiastic response—and this connection will come in handy later if you run into trouble and need some TECHNICAL HELP.

Living in the Material World

One of the most compelling reasons for jumping on the knitting bandwagon is the amazing abundance of fabulous knitting materials available from knitting shops, craft chains, and online suppliers.

It's a Big Yarn-iverse Out There!

If you're like most knitting novices, you are chomping at the bit to run out and purchase bags full of novelty yarns (the ones with all the texture), bulky yarns (yes, the big fat ones), and luxury fibers (like cashmere, angora, and alpaca). Be patient, though. We recommend learning with a basic yarn—it's easier to work with, doesn't split, and is more forgiving. And, choose a light color—it's easier to see. You'll soon learn that yarn is organized by weight (thickness) and ranges from super-fine to super-bulky. For your first project, we recommend a worsted or mid-weight yarn. Nearly all yarn comes with a ball band or label clearly stating the recommended needle size and gauge (more on that later). Always save the ball band as it is the source of lots more useful information, including fiber content and care instructions. Speaking of balls, most commercial yarn you'll run across will be in the form of a ball (round) or skein (oblong), with the yarn pulling out from the center. Occasionally you'll find a yarn you love that's "put up" in hank form, which will have to be rolled into a ball. If the yarn shop can't do it for you, enlist a friend (or kid) to act as a human "niddy noddy" (hank holder) while you wind the ball.

You'll Need Needles

Knitting needles come in a wide variety of materials. Traditional metal needles make that classic knitting "click" that remind many of us of Grandma but can be cold to the touch. Plastic needles are lightweight and widely available. Today the favorites of most middle-aged knitters seem to be wood and bam-

boo needles, which have a warm, earthy feel to them, and the rounded ends don't split the yarn. Bamboo is flexible and the needles warm up as you work with them. Wooden needles, available in everything from birch to ebony, are elegant to the eye and pleasing to the touch but tend to be pricey. It's a good idea to experiment and see which material feels most comfortable to you.

In knitting, size matters, and knitting needles range in thickness from absurdly tiny (for making socks or fine lace) to awkwardly huge (for working with mega-bulky yarns). The size of the needle corresponds with the size of the yarn and is indicated on the ball band of the yarn. Needles usually come in a couple of lengths, too, 10" and 14" being the most common.

Shed a Little Light (and Magnification) on the Subject

Don't let declining eyesight keep you from picking up the needles. Consider investing in a daylight-simulating floor or table lamp. Natural light is the most relaxing for the eyes and allows you to work for longer periods of time. And let's face it, you're not always going to be sitting in the sunroom to knit. Luckily, there are attractive lamps on the market so your living room won't look like an operating room. Even lamps with detachable magnifiers are available. But if you prefer the "leave a pair of glasses on every table" approach, upgrade from drugstore reading glasses to a pair (or several) of optical-grade spectacles, available in styles so glamorous you'll want a pair for every surface! Most important, please avoid eyestrain. Take frequent breaks, close your eyes from time to time, and try "palming" (gently rest palms on closed eyes for a few moments). And, yes, drink plenty of water—it helps keep eyes lubricated.

Oh, My Aching Hands!

One common concern is whether knitting will trigger repetitive stress conditions, such as carpal tunnel syndrome, or will aggravate arthritis. According to Shannon Whetstone Mescher, spokesperson for the Arthritis Foundation, knitting doesn't cause arthritis, nor does it make it worse. In fact, she suggests you check with your physician if your condition is severe, but says, "The benefits of movement, especially keeping joints lubricated, usually outweigh the downside." She recommends frequent breaks, hand stretches, and massage. For the most part, the same applies to carpal tunnel sufferers. However, folks with constant hand pain from either condition might want to try specially designed fingerless support gloves. Available at craft stores, massage gloves support and warm the hands to minimize fatigue, pain, and swelling.

Speaking of hands, if your hands tend to be dry (whose aren't?), be sure to use a rich, emollient hand cream to keep your skin from cracking. Keep a nail file "on hand" for smoothing rough nails and preventing snags in your yarn. In case you were wondering: Although sheep's wool contains lanolin, an ingredient in many hand creams (knitters of yesteryear had the softest of hands), most of today's yarns have been cleaned so thoroughly that they contain only a trace of skin-softening lanolin.

Organizing Principles

Once you have a few knitting projects underway, you'll undoubtedly realize you need a system for curbing yarn chaos. One way to add method to your newfound madness is to initiate the "tote bag system" of organization—a separate, very cute bag for each project you've begun, containing yarn (don't forget to save the ball bands), needles, and the pattern you are using. Keep your pattern in a plastic sleeve for protection as you knit. When you're done with the project, insert the pattern into a loose-leaf binder or knitting notebook along with other vital info pertaining to that project—yarn ball bands, a note of where you bought the yarn, and a snapshot of the recipient. You'll be able to look back and see what you made and for whom—very handy in the event of a memory lapse. Many knitting shops sell a variety of knitter's journals designed especially for keeping a record of completed projects. And, speaking of memory lapses, store needles in a fabric needle holder, organized by size, also available in yarn stores. That way each time you need size 10 needles, you won't be tempted to run out to buy another pair because you can't remember where you put them.

More Tools of the Trade

When you're first learning to knit, there's not much you need besides knitting needles and a couple balls of yarn. Once you move on to more advanced projects, however, you may find some of these inexpensive gadgets infinitely helpful:

1 Small sharp scissors for snipping off loose yarn ends

2 Large-eyed, blunt-tipped yarn- or tapestry needles for seaming and weaving in yarn ends

3 Flexible, non-stretch tape measure, good for measuring the length of those scarves, but essential when you start knitting sweaters

4 An assortment of pins—rust-proof T-pins for blocking, straight pins for seaming, and safety pins for marking rows

5 A variety of crochet hooks, handy for picking up dropped stitches as well as adding decorative trim to knitted items

6 A plastic or metal stitch gauge—more on that when we discuss gauge in Chapter 3: Next Steps.

7 Double-pointed cable needles that hold stitches while you work a cable pattern.

(You'll need a few other items for blocking your first project, but we'll get to that in Chapter 4: A Fine Finish.)

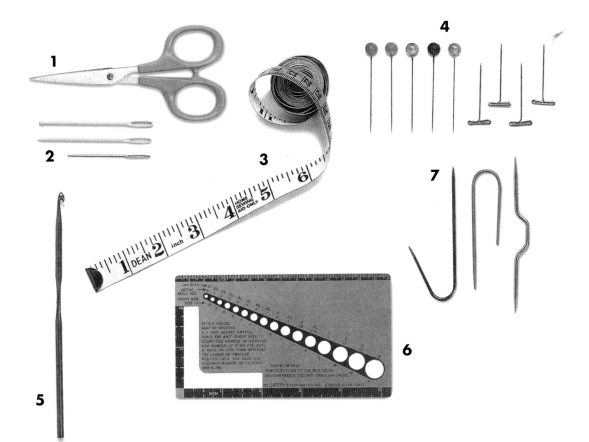

Please Be Seated

Before you begin knitting, pay attention to where you'll be sitting. A brief survey of some knitters in their prime (in other words, well aware of the aches and pains of middle age) resulted in these two words: lumbar support! There's no need to go out and buy a high-end, ergonomic, designer chair. But, if you're going to be knitting for any length of time, sit in a firm armchair, and please don't slouch!

Let the Fun Begin!

English or Continental? (No, it's not your choice of breakfasts!)

One of the biggest frustrations for a new knitter of any age is finding the most comfortable way to hold the yarn and needles. With just a little time and patience, your hands will fall into a comfortable rhythm. Learning to hold the yarn and needles is a bit confusing, mostly because no two people do it the same way. The two main styles of knitting are English and Continental. Though both create the same end product, most knitters have very specific opinions about which way is superior (their way, of course!). Here's the major difference: English knitters hold and "throw" the yarn with their right hand, while Continental knitters manipulate the yarn with their left hand. Folks with arthritis or carpal tunnel syndrome should be especially conscious of which method feels most comfortable to them.

Once you've decided which hand will hold the working yarn, there's still one more decision to make—how to hold the needles. Some knitters like to grasp their needles over the top, while others would rather hold them like pencils, resting the majority of the needle between the thumb and index finger. There is honestly no right or wrong way to accomplish this, so experiment with the different choices. You will soon develop your own unique style.

Be prepared for a little awkwardness in the beginning. Give yourself plenty of time to get comfortable with the new hand positions and motions involved in knitting. With a little time and patience, you'll soon have all the grandkids in fancy new sweaters!

Casting On

There are many ways to get those initial stitches on the needle. We have selected two of the simplest, most sturdy, and neatly attractive versions to start with. The first, a double cast-on, will use one needle and two lengths of yarn. Our second method, the knit-on variation, uses two needles and one strand of yarn.

A solid cast-on row leads to good results. The best way to perfect this method is to practice casting on, using your favorite method or technique, until it becomes an easy process for you.

It's possible that when you first start to cast on, your foundation row will be so tight that it'll be tricky to get your needle through those little loops. If you have this problem, attempt casting on with two needles held together or using a needle two sizes larger than you'll be using for the remainder of the project.

Slip Knot

The slip knot is the beginning of the process—it anchors the yarn to the needles and makes casting on possible. Before you begin the slip knot, decide which method of casting on to try. For the double cast-on method, leave about an inch of yarn for every stitch that you want to place on the needle. If you choose the knit-on cast-on method, leave eight to ten inches between the end of the yarn and the slip knot.

Slip Knot

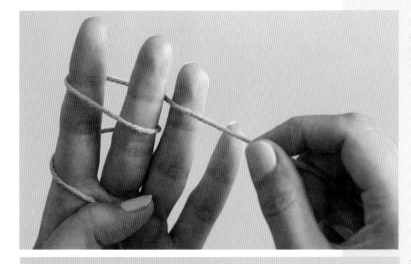

1. Hold the short end of the yarn in your palm with your thumb. Wrap the yarn twice around the index and middle fingers.

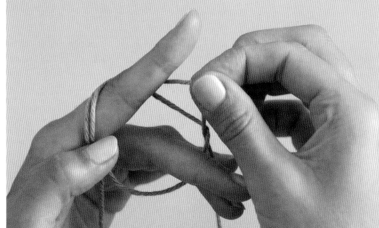

2. Pull the strand attached to the ball through the loop between your two fingers, forming a new loop.

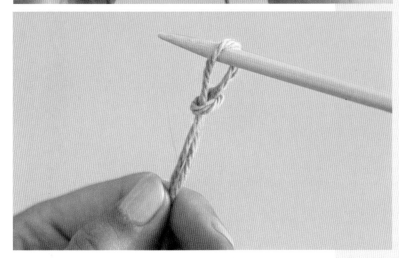

3. Place the new loop on the needle. Tighten the loop on the needle by pulling on both ends of the yarn to form the slip knot. You are now ready to begin casting on.

1. Make a slip knot on the right needle, leaving a long tail. Wind the tail-end around your left thumb, front to back. Wrap the yarn from the ball over your left index finger and secure the ends in your palm.

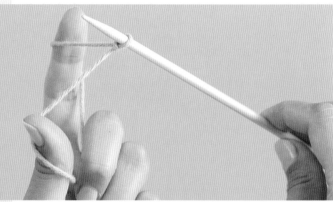

2. Insert the needle upward in the loop on your thumb.

3. With the needle, draw the yarn from the ball through the loop to form a stitch. Take your thumb out of the loop and tighten the loop on the needle. Continue in this way until the all the stitches are cast on.

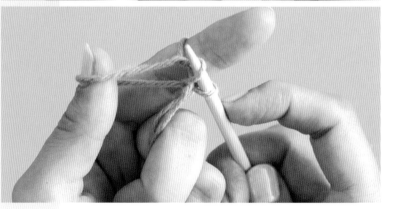

1. Make a slip knot on the left needle. *Insert the right needle knitwise into the stitch on the left needle. Wrap the yarn around the right needle as if to knit.

2. Draw the yarn through the first stitch to make a new stitch, but do not drop the first stitch from the left needle.

3. Slip the new stitch to the left needle as shown. Repeat from the * (in step 1) until the required number of stitches is cast on.

Knit Stitch

After you are comfortable with the cast on, you can begin knitting. There are two different ways to make each knit stitch (English or Continental method). What you choose depends on your own comfort.

It may take some time to feel at ease, but keep working at it and it'll get easier. If you have any friends at yarn shops or knitting clubs, this is a good time to stay in touch. Being in contact with an experienced knitter will make the learning process easier.

1. Hold the needle with the cast-on stitches in your left hand. Hold the working needle in your right hand, wrapping the yarn around your fingers. Insert the right needle from front to back into the first cast-on stitch on the left needle. Keep the right needle under the left needle and the yarn at the back.

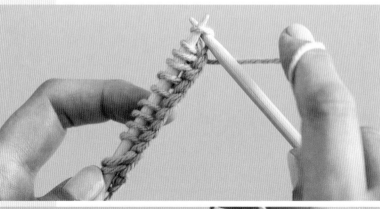

2. Wrap the yarn under and over the right needle in a clockwise motion.

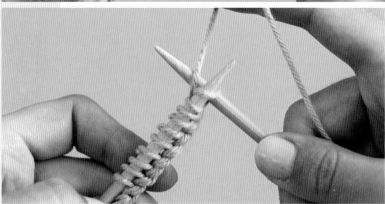

3. With the right needle, catch the yarn and pull it through the cast-on stitch.

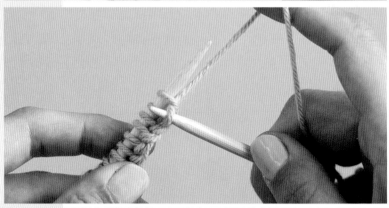

4. Slip the cast-on stitch off the left needle, leaving the newly formed stitch on the right needle. Repeat these steps in each subsequent stitch until all stitches have been worked from the left needle. You have made one row of knit stitches.

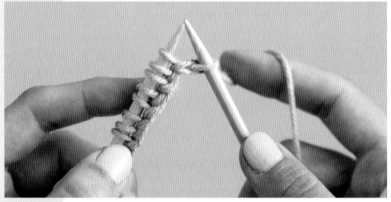

Knit Stitch: Continental

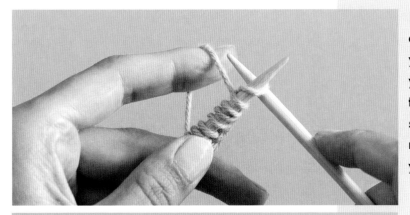

1. Hold the needles in the same way as the English method, but hold the yarn with your left hand rather than your right. Insert the right needle from front to back into the first cast-on stitch on the left needle. Keep the right needle under the left needle, with the yarn at the back.

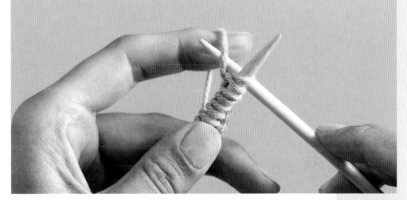

2. Lay the yarn over the right needle as shown.

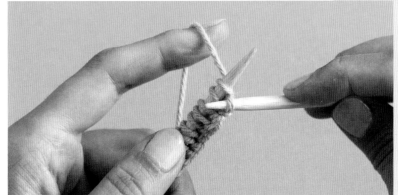

3. With the tip of the right needle, pull the strand through the cast-on stitch, holding the strand with the right index finger if necessary.

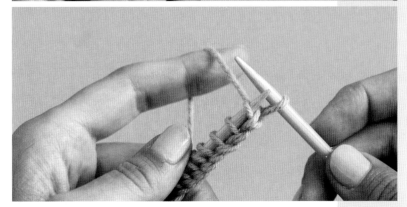

4. Slip the cast-on stitch off the left needle, leaving the newly formed stitch on the right needle. Continue to repeat these steps until you have worked all of the stitches from the left needle to the right needle. You have made one row of knit stitches.

The garter stitch is the simplest of all stitch patterns and is completed by knitting every row. The end result will be a flat, reversible, ridged fabric that will stand up well to wear and will not roll at the edges.

After you reach the end of the first row of knit stitches, move the full needle to your left hand and begin knitting each stitch all over again. Once you have completed several rows, you'll start to see the results. As you get deeper into the project, your growing strip of garter stitch will begin to look like a real piece of knitted fabric.

Purl Stitch

Take a breather and exercise those fingers. You will now learn an extremely important stitch in the world of knitting: the purl stitch. In reality, purling is just a backward version of knitting. When you put knitting and purling together, you can come up with literally hundreds of stitch patterns. Some people find the purl stitch more complicated than the knit stitch (which is why the knit stitch is taught first). If you don't master it early on, just remember practice makes perfect. Once you understand how to purl, it will feel completely natural.

Purl Stitch: English

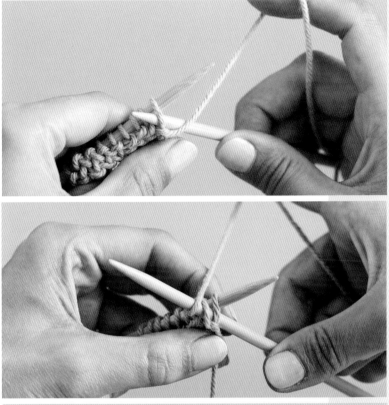

1. As with the knit stitch, hold the working needle in your right hand and the needle with the stitches in your left. The yarn is held and manipulated with your right hand and is kept to the front of the work. Insert the right needle from back to front into the first stitch on the left needle. The right needle is now in front of the left needle, and the yarn is at the front of the work.

2. With your right index finger, wrap the yarn counterclockwise around the right needle.

3. Draw the right needle and the yarn backward through the stitch on the left needle, forming a loop on the right needle.

4. Slip the stitch off the left needle. You have made one purl stitch. Repeat these steps in each subsequent stitch until all stitches have been worked from the left needle. You have made one row of purl stitches.

1. As with the knit stitch, hold the working needle in your right hand and the needle with the stitches in your left. The yarn is held and manipulated with your left hand and is kept to the front of the work. Insert the right needle from back to front into the first stitch on the left needle, keeping the yarn in front of the work.

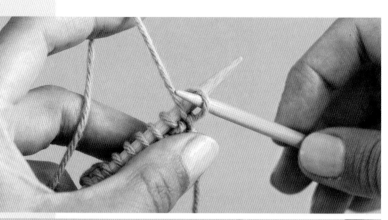

2. Lay the yarn over the right needle as shown. Pull down on the yarn with your left index finger to keep the yarn taut.

3. Bring the right needle and the yarn backward through the stitch on the left needle, forming a loop on the right needle.

4. Slide the stitch off the left needle. Use your left index finger to tighten the new purl stitch on the right needle. Continue to repeat these steps until you have worked all of the stitches from the left needle to the right needle. You have made one row of purl stitches.

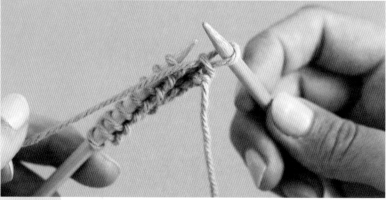

Stockinette Stitch

Knit and purl stitches can be combined to create the stockinette stitch, the beautiful V-patterned fabric that people most often associate with knitting.

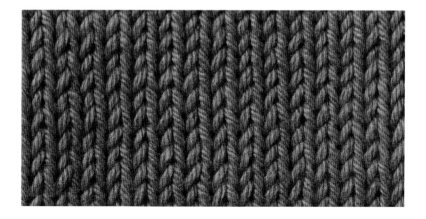

Binding Off

After you are finished with your knitting, you will need to bind off your stitches so that your project will not unravel. Binding off is not complicated, but watch for tension. If you bind off too tightly, you will create a pucker on top. To prevent this, try binding off with a needle two sizes larger than you used for the rest of the project.

1. Knit two stitches. *Insert the left needle into the first stitch on the right needle.

2. Pull this stitch over the second stitch and off the right needle.

3. One stitch remains on the right needle as shown. Knit the next stitch. Repeat from the * (in step 1) until you have bound off the required number of stitches.

Joining Yarn

Soon enough, you will be knitting along and realize that your yarn ball is looking smaller and smaller. Don't panic—it's simply time to join yarn!

Joining yarn works best at the end of a row. That way, it will be easier to weave in your ends without creating too much of a bulge. Simply tie the new yarn loosely around the old yarn, leaving at least a 6" (15cm) tail. Then untie the knot and weave in the ends.

To change yarn in the middle of a row, simply poke your right needle into the next stitch, but wrap the new yarn around the needle in place of the old yarn and keep on knitting. After you've reached the end of a row, tie the old and new strands together so that they don't unravel.

Weaving in Ends

When the time comes that you finish up a ball of yarn, you'll discover you have loose ends. In order to hide those strands and create a product that truly looks finished, you must weave the loose ends into the wrong side of the knitted fabric.

To begin, carefully untie the knot you made when first joining new yarn. Then take a loose strand and thread it through the yarn needle, snaking the needle (and attached yarn) down through approximately five of the free loops along the edge of your knitting. Remember to snip close to the work to remove whatever's left, but be careful not to cut into the actual knitting. Then thread the second strand through the needle and weave up.

If you need to change the yarn in the middle of a row, untie the knot and weave one loose piece in each direction horizontally, following the path of the affected stitch through five or six additional stitches on the wrong side of the work. You should always double-check the right side of the fabric to make sure no puckering or slackness has cropped in.

Chapter three: Next steps

Beginner or no, there's MORE to knitting than baby steps.

Once you have created scarves to your heart's content, and made blankets for all of the babies among your friends and family, it's time to ADVANCE to shaping. These techniques are simple, and learning them will open you up to NEW HORIZONS. Reading schematics, ribbing, and stitch gauges, too, are important. You're almost ready for the world of SWEATER MAKING!

Less Is More: Decreasing

Decreasing (or reducing the number of stitches in a row) is a method of creating shaping within a knitting piece. Two of the easiest and most common decreases are the knit two together (or k2tog) and purl two together (or p2tog) decreases. These basic decreases slant to the right on the knit side of the work.

K2TOG: Insert the right needle from front to back (knitwise) into the next two stitches on the left needle. Wrap the yarn around the right needle (as when knitting) and pull it through. You have decreased one stitch.

P2TOG: Insert the right needle into the front loops (purlwise) of the next two stitches on the left needle. Wrap the yarn around the right needle (as when purling) and pull it through. You have decreased one stitch.

Increasing Opportunities!

Increasing also changes the number of stitches. As with decreasing, there are various ways to do it. The bar increase, which is made by working in the front and back loops of the same stitch, is extremely common.

Bar Increase

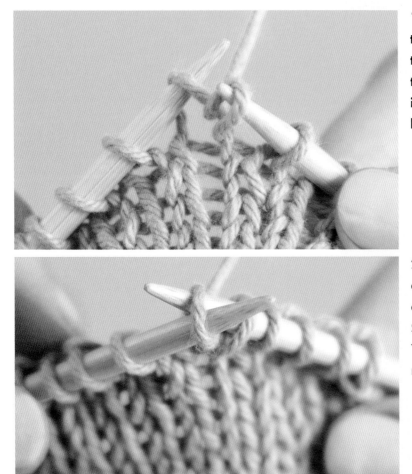

1. To increase on the knit side, insert the right needle knitwise into the stitch to be increased. Wrap the yarn around the right needle and pull it through as if knitting, but leave the stitch on the left needle.

2. Insert the right needle into the back of the same stitch. Wrap the yarn around the needle and pull it through. Slip the stitch off the left needle. You now have two stitches on the right needle.

Working in Front and Back Loops

The loop closest to you is the front of the stitch. This is the loop you'll normally work into. To knit into the front loop, insert the right needle from left to right into the stitch on the left needle. To purl into the front loop, insert needle from right to left into the stitch.

To knit into the back loop (loop farthest from you), insert the right needle from right to left under left needle and into the stitch. To purl into the back loop, insert needle from behind into the stitch.

Knitting into the back loop

Purling into the back loop

Make a Ribbing

The popular stockinette stitch is created by alternating whole rows of knit and purl stitches. However, it's also possible to switch back and forth within the same row to create many different patterns.

Ribbing is the most popular knit/purl stitch. It is stretchy and has the ability to "bounce" back into place, making ribbing ideal for hems, necks, and cuffs of most sweaters. In ribbing, you can make a total garment—ribbed sweaters create a slimming effect that any wearer would love. There'll be more about ribbing in Chapter 5: A Basic Stitch Sampler.

Hint: For beginners, the trickiest part about ribbing is remembering to shift the yarn back and forth when working the different stitches. In k2p2 ribbing, you knit two stitches, move the yarn between the two needles to the front of the work, and then purl two stitches. When you are ready to knit again, return the yarn to the back of the work by passing it between the two needles, then continue with your pattern. If yarn isn't shifted from back to front and front to back between knit and purl stitches, you will end up with extra stitches on your needle and a rectangular piece that will quickly resemble a triangle.

Basic Ribbing (Moving Yarn Back and Forth)

When knitting a stitch, as you've probably noticed by now, the yarn is always held at the back of the work. However, in purling, the yarn is always at the front. With ribbing, when you move from a knit to a purl stitch, you must be sure the yarn is in the correct position to work the next stitch. When you are moving the yarn from the back to the front, or vice versa, the yarn should go between the two needles, and not over them.

Yarn in back

Yarn in front

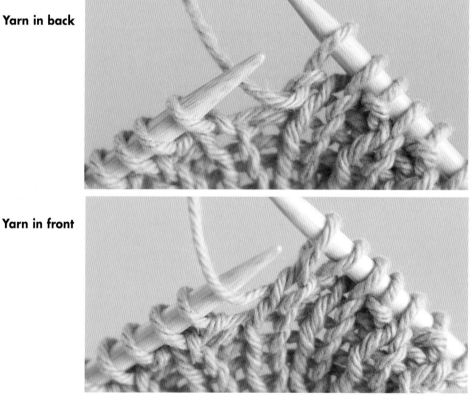

Get in Gauge

The gauge swatch is the first step in garment making. The gauge swatch is a square piece of knitted fabric that demonstrates how you, the needles, and the yarn interact before you get going on the main project. You will find a recommended gauge, or stitches and rows per inch, at the beginning of the instructions on every project, usually directly beneath the suggestions for yarn weight and needle size.

To create the gauge swatch, gather the exact yarn and needles that you plan to use for your project (even the smallest differences such as yarn color and needle brand can affect your gauge). Cast on a number of stitches that will give you at least four inches across, and then work in stockinette stitch or the specified stitch pattern until you have made a bit more than four vertical inches of fabric.

These two squares of knitting illustrate the importance of the gauge swatch. Each swatch is made with an identical number of stitches and rows, but the one on the left uses a smaller needle size than the one on the right. Are you inspired to make a gauge swatch before starting a whole garment? We hope so!

You can measure your gauge swatches with a tape measure. Or, you can make use of a stitch gauge (see page 43) in the center of your swatch, and count the stitches and rows inside the two-inch (5 cm) right-angle opening.

Now, merely remove the needle from the stitches (without binding off) and put the sample on a flat, smooth surface like a hardwood floor or kitchen table. Using a tape measure, ruler, or stitch gauge, measure across four inches of the knitting in both directions and count the number of stitches within those four inches (don't forget fractions of stitches). If you have more stitches to the inch than the pattern instructs, go up one needle size. If you have fewer stitches than recommended, try again with a smaller needle.

When you are as near as achievable to the recommended gauge, go ahead and begin knitting your garment, but don't forget about gauge in general just yet.

You can make the gauge swatch easier to work with by including selvage stitches on the edges of the square. Selvage stitches help the piece of fabric lay nice and flat, as well as making measuring easier, by giving you clear-cut edges between which to measure. To craft selvage stitches, work two rows of garter stitch (knit every row) at the top and bottom of the swatch and include two stitches in garter stitch at the beginning and end of each stockinette row.

At times, the gauge of your actual garment may change dramatically from the gauge of your original swatch. After you've worked about 5" (12 cm) of the first piece of your project, recheck your gauge by laying the piece down on a flat surface and pulling out your tape measure (or stitch gauge) again. Your knitting should be as near to the suggested gauge as it was before. In the event that it's not, you'll have to unravel what you've done and start again using a different needle size. As you rip out the rows and roll the yarn back into a ball, remember it is better to do this now and have a usable garment in the long run.

Tip: Knitters sometimes mistakenly believe that creating the gauge swatch is an extra, unnecessary step that can be avoided altogether. This is not true. Always make the gauge swatch! Let's say your knitting is one half inch off of suggested gauge—your whole garment can end up unwearable! There's nothing quite as frustrating as working diligently on an adult's hat that ends up being the size of a toddler's, or making a baby's hat that would fit a grown man.

What on Earth Is a "Stitch Gauge"?

A stitch gauge is a flat rectangle of metal or plastic that simplifies the process of measuring gauge by providing a little window through which you can easily count stitches. First, lay your knitting down on a flat surface and then line up the L-shaped window with the corner of a stitch. Count the number of Vs in the window (both horizontally and vertically) to get accurate stitch and row gauges.

Another feature of stitch gauges is a row of holes that can be used to identify the size of unmarked needles. To do this, slip the needle into holes of

increasing size until you reach a hole that lets the needle pass all the way through. The hole's corresponding number is your needle's size.

For Short: Knitting Abbreviations

As you begin using knitting patterns, you will see that they seem to be written in a completely different language. For instance, what on earth does "*K1, p1; rep from *" mean? These confusing groups of letters, numbers, and symbols are part of a system of knitting terminology that saves space in patterns and makes instructions less boring to read. Here, we list and describe the terms you'll run across in this book.

Grasping Schematics

When you reach the end of most sweater patterns, you will find line drawings with bullets and numbers skirting the sides, and words like "Back" and "Left Front" scrawled across the centers. These are called schematics, and have some very important uses in our task at hand.

The first thing to remember is schematics are drawn to scale. They give you an at-a-glance rundown of all the measurements, angles, and shapes of the sweater you're making. Schematics will also reveal if the sweater tapers at the waist or narrows at the shoulders, and indicate the exact depth and width of the armholes, bust, and sleeves. The most thrilling thing about schematics is that they provide you with a small idea of what your sweater pieces will look like when completed. Hint: When blocking your finished garment, schematics will be very useful (see Chapter 4: A Fine Finish).

In general, the simpler the sweater, the simpler the schematic. The drawings on this page are good examples of schematics for a beginner-level woman's pullover sweater. The numbers preceding the parentheses represent the smallest size, while the numbers inside the parentheses indicate measurements for sequentially increasing sizes.

Knitting Abbreviations

approx   approximately

beg   begin, beginning

ch 1   chain one (crochet loop)

cont   continue

dec   decrease

dpn   double-pointed needle(s)

in/cm/mm   inches/centimeters/millimeters

inc   increase

inc (dec)…sts evenly across row   Count the number of stitches in the row, and then divide that number by the number of stitches to be increased (decreased). The result of this division will tell you how many stitches to work between each increased (decreased) stitch.

k   knit

k the knit and p the purl sts   This is a phrase used when a pattern of knit and purl stitches has been established and will be continued for some time. When the stitch that's facing you looks like a V, knit it. When it looks like a bump, purl it.

k2tog   knit two together (a method of decreasing explained on page 36)

k3tog   knit three together (worked same as k2tog, but insert needle into 3 sts instead of 2 for a double decrease)

knitwise   Insert the needle into the stitch as if you were going to knit it.

m1   With the needle tip, lift the strand between the last stitch knit and the next stitch on the lefthand needle and knit into the back of it. One knit stitch has been added.

oz/g   ounces/grams (usually in reference to amount of yarn in a single ball)

p   purl

p2tog   purl two together (a method of decreasing explained on page 36)

pat   pattern

pm   place marker

purlwise   Insert the needle into the stitch as if you were going to purl it.

rem   remain, remains, or remaining

rep   repeat

rep from *   Repeat the instructions after the asterisk as many times as indicated. If the directions say "rep from * to end," continue to repeat the instructions after the asterisk to the end of the row.

rev sc   reverse single crochet

reverse shaping   A term used for garments like cardigans where shaping for the right and left fronts is identical, but reversed. For example, neck edge stitches decreased at the beginning of the row for the first piece will be decreased at the end of the row on the second. In general, follow the directions for the first piece, being sure to mirror the decreases (increases) on each side.

RS   right side

sc   single crochet

SKP   Slip one stitch knitwise to right-hand needle. Knit the next stitch and pass the slipped stitch over the knit stitch.

SK2P   Slip one stitch, knit two stitches together, pass slipped stitch over the two stitches knit together.

sl st   slip stitch (crochet)

slip   Transfer the indicated stitches from the left to the right needle without working (knitting or purling) them.

Small (Medium, Large)   The most common method of displaying changes in pattern for different sizes. In general, the measurements, stitch counts, directions, etc. for the smallest size come first, followed by the increasingly larger sizes in parentheses. When there is only one number given, it applies to all of the sizes.

ssk   slip one, slip one, k2tog

St st   stockinette stitch

st/sts   stitch/stitches

work even   Continue in the established pattern without working any increases or decreases.

WS   wrong side

wyib   with yarn in back

yo   yarn over

When making a cardigan, the schematics are like those for a pullover sweater, but the front is different. For cardigans, one of the two front pieces will be drawn, and then you just have to visualize (or sketch) a mirror image for the other. That's not so hard, right?

Oops! A Quick-Fix Guide to Correcting Mistakes

As a knitter, you will make a mistake from time to time—we all do. However, as long as you know how to fix those mistakes, it's no big deal. Here, we've outlined (and explained how to fix) some of the most frequent errors that plague beginners as well as veterans in the knitting world.

picking up a dropped *purl* stitch

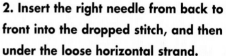

Purl Side

1. This method is used when a purl stitch has been dropped only one row. Work to the dropped purl stitch. Be sure that the loose horizontal strand is in front of the dropped stitch.

2. Insert the right needle from back to front into the dropped stitch, and then under the loose horizontal strand.

3. With the left needle, lift the dropped stitch over the horizontal strand and off the right needle.

4. Transfer the newly made purl stitch back to the left needle by inserting the left needle from front to back into the stitch and slipping it off the right needle.

Knit Side

1. This method is used when a knit stitch has been dropped only one row. Work to where the stitch was dropped. Be sure that the loose strand is behind the dropped stitch.

2. Insert the right needle from front to back into the dropped stitch and under the loose horizontal strand behind.

3. Insert the left needle from the back into the dropped stitch on the right needle, and pull this stitch over the loose strand.

4. Transfer this newly made stitch back to the left needle by inserting the left needle from front to back into the stitch and slipping it off the right needle.

an extra knit stitch at the end

Knit Side

If you bring the yarn back over the top of the needle at the beginning of the knit row, the first stitch will have two loops instead of one, as shown.

To avoid creating this extra stitch, keep the yarn under the needle when taking it to the back to knit the first stitch.

Purl Side

At the beginning of a purl row, if the yarn is at the back, and then brought to the front under the needle, the first stitch will have two loops instead of one, as shown.

To avoid making these two loops, the yarn should be at the front before you purl the first stitch.

Chapter four: A fine finish

It is always essential in KNITTING to tie up
loose ends—that goes for LIFE, too!

At least with knitting, the process involves only a few simple steps: blocking (shaping the pieces you've knit), sewing those pieces together, and weaving in all the loose ends. We'll also show you some lovely FINISHING TOUCHES, such as how to make buttonholes. Soon you'll be whipping up some very professional-looking sweaters. Dear knitters, you are entering the HOME STRETCH.

New Kids on the Block

Sometimes, the freshly knit garment may appear wavy and misshapen. Blocking has taught us a lesson: Yarn is very forgiving. Colors and patterns may be more fun, but without blocking, even a perfectly knit garment wouldn't look right. So, please, pull out that blocking equipment (see below) and follow along as we teach you how to mold your already-beautiful pieces into shape.

Wet and steam are the two main methods of blocking. The Pressing Guide (page 54) will help you discover which is best for your project. But before beginning either method, gather up any schematics or measurements from the pattern, and use them like architectural plans. Then you will know exactly how far the pieces should stretch and where they should dip and swell.

What You'll Need:

1 Flat, covered, padded surface large enough to hold one piece of knitting (for example, carpet or bed covered with plastic and a towel)

2 Rust-proof T-pins (NOT pins with little plastic colored heads—these will melt during steam blocking, creating a huge mess)

3 Tape measure

4 Spray bottle with cool water (or basin full of cool water) or steam iron (or handheld steamer)

5 Towels (be sure they're colorfast)

6 Pressing cloth

Pinning and Blocking

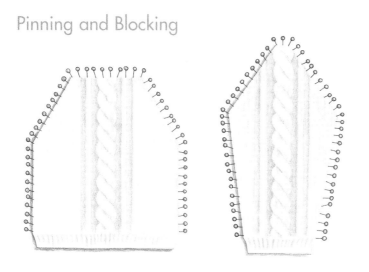

1. Pin the key areas as shown

2. Pin the piece evenly, omitting the ribbing

Wet Blocking For wet blocking, immerse the knitted pieces in cool water, squeeze them out, and stretch them on a flat board to their exact measurements according to the schematics. Or you can pin the pieces first and then wet them down with a water-filled spray bottle. Your personal preference will determine the method you use, though you may find the spraying method to be less awkward. Once the pieces are wet, leave them there until they are completely dry. This may take 24 hours or more, so be patient.

Steam Blocking For steam blocking, first pin the pieces on a flat surface according to the schematics. Fire up your steam iron or hand-held steamer, and when it's nice and steamy, hold the iron close to the fabric until the fabric is convincingly damp. Never touch the iron to the stitches! If you must press lightly, protect your knitted investment of time and money by sandwiching a colorfast towel or pressing cloth between the fabric and the hot metal. As with wet blocking, leave the pieces to dry completely. Drying time after steaming probably won't take as long as it does for wet blocking, but you may still need to be patient for several hours. While waiting, you can plan your next sweater!

Fibers will react differently to heat, so it is best to know what to expect before you press or steam them. Remember that there are many combinations of fibers. You should choose the process that is well-suited to all the components of the garment. If you are unsure about the fiber content of your yarn, test your gauge swatch before blocking your sweater pieces.

Angora Wet block by spraying.

Cotton Wet block or warm/hot steam press.

Linen Wet block or warm/hot steam press.

Lurex Do not block.

Mohair Wet block by spraying.

Novelties Do not block.

Synthetics Carefully follow instructions on ball band—usually wet block by spraying. Do not press.

Wool and all wool-like fibers (alpaca, camel hair, cashmere) Wet block by spraying or warm steam press.

Wool blends Wet block by spraying; do not press unless tested.

Seams Like a Dream

After the last strand of every piece of your garment has been finished, there's one thing left to do to make your pieces wearable: Sew them together. Sewing together, or "seaming," is achieved with a yarn needle and the same yarn used to make your project.

Sewing together knitted fabric can be done in many different ways, with each method serving a different purpose. One kind of seaming is best for joining adjacent lengths of stockinette stitch, and another is better for connecting vertical and horizontal pieces of the same fabric. Pattern instructions usually recommend a particular method to use, so just follow the directions, and your project will come out beautifully.

Make sure you have correctly lined up those little stitches before sewing those seams. Find the cast-on stitches on both sides. Pin the stitches together with a straight pin or safety pin. Count up ten rows on each side and pin the corresponding stitches together. Continue until you get to the top of the two pieces. When creating a garment like a hat, the rows should line up exactly. If you end up with extra rows on one side, go back and see where some stragglers might have occurred on the opposite side. If you are seaming two separate pieces, you may have to ease in extra rows if one piece is slightly longer than the other.

How to Begin Seaming

If there is a long tail left from your cast-on row, use this strand to begin sewing. To make a neat join at the lower edge with no gap, use the technique shown here.

Thread the strand into a yarn needle. With the right sides of both pieces facing you, insert the yarn needle from back to front into the corner stitch of the piece without the tail. Making a figure eight with the yarn, insert the needle from back to front into the stitch with the cast-on tail. Tighten to close the gap.

Vertical Seam on Stockinette Stitch

The vertical seam is worked from the right side and is used to join two edges row by row. It hides the uneven stitches at the edge of a row and creates an invisible seam, making the knitting appear continuous.

Insert the yarn needle under the horizontal bar between the first and second stitches. Insert the needle into the corresponding bar on the other piece. Continue alternating from side to side.

Vertical Seam on Garter Stitch

This seam joins two edges row by row like vertical seaming on stockinette stitch. The alternating pattern of catching top and bottom stitch loops makes the join nearly invisible.

Insert the yarn needle into the top loop on one side, then in the bottom loop of the corresponding stitch on the other side. Continue to alternate in this way.

Horizontal Seam on Stockinette Stitch

This seam is used to join two bound-off edges, such as for shoulder seams or hoods, and is worked stitch by stitch. You must have the same number of stitches on each piece so that the finished seam will resemble a continuous row of knit stitches. Be sure to pull the yarn tight enough to hide the bound-off edges.

With the bound-off edges together, lined up stitch for stitch, insert the yarn needle under a stitch inside the bound-off edge of one side and then under the corresponding stitch on the other side. Repeat all the way across the join.

Vertical to Horizontal Seam

Used to connect a bound-off edge to a vertical length of knitted fabric, this seam requires careful pre-measuring and marking to ensure an even seam.

Insert the needle under one or two horizontal bars between the first and second stitches of the horizontal piece. Shown here on stockinette stitch.

Pick Up Lines

Sometimes you will need to "pick up stitches." Although this might sound like a children's game, once you get the hang of it, it's as easy as pie. One picks up stitches with a knitting needle or crochet hook and a new strand of yarn, dipping into and out of the edge of the knitted fabric, creating new loops. These new loops will serve as the foundation for a collar, button band, sleeve, or baby bootie instep.

For picking up stitches along a straight edge, focus on the two S's: side and spacing. For the first "S," be sure to pick up stitches with the right side facing out. The second "S" reminds you to space the stitches evenly along the fabric. Make sure that the loops you pick up aren't clustered together or separated by vast expanses along the knitted edge.

Picking Up Along a Bound-off Edge

1. Insert the knitting needle into the corner stitch of the first row, one stitch in from the side edge. Wrap the yarn around the needle knitwise.

2. Draw the yarn through. You have picked up one stitch. Continue to pick up stitches along the edge. Occasionally skip one row to keep the edge from flaring.

The Hole Truth

Have you ever looked at perfectly created holes in cardigans and wondered how the knitter made them? We are about to teach you. We will study the two-row horizontal buttonhole, the one-row horizontal buttonhole, and the yarn-over buttonhole. The two-row and one-row buttonholes are shown worked over four stitches, though you might want to use more or less depending on the size of your button.

Two-Row Horizontal Buttonhole

The most common buttonhole is undoubtedly the two-row horizontal buttonhole, probably because you can easily make it fit your button. Make it by binding off a number of stitches on one row and casting them on again on the next. The last stitch bound off is part of the left side of the buttonhole.

1. On the first row, work to the placement of the buttonhole. Knit two, with the left needle, pull one stitch over the other stitch, *knit one, pull the second stitch over the knit one; repeat from the * twice more. Four stitches have been bound off.

2. On the next row, work to the bound-off stitches and cast on four stitches. On the next row, work these stitches through the back loops to tighten them.

One-Row Horizontal Buttonhole

The one-row horizontal buttonhole is the neatest buttonhole and requires no further reinforcing. Although it's slightly more complicated than the two-row horizontal buttonhole, the extra effort produces a fantastic, super-clean result.

1. Work to the buttonhole, bring yarn to front, and slip a stitch purlwise. Place yarn at back and leave it there. *Slip next stitch from left needle. Pass the first slipped stitch over it; repeat from the * three times more (not moving yarn). Slip the last bound-off stitch to the left needle and turn work.

2. Using the cable cast on with the yarn at the back, cast on five stitches as follows: *Insert the right needle between the first and second stitches on the left needle, draw up a loop, place the loop on the left needle; repeat from the * four times more, turn the work.

3. Slip the first stitch with the yarn in back from the left needle and pass the extra cast-on stitch over it to close the buttonhole. Work to the end of the row.

Yarn-Over Buttonhole

If you are creating a smaller, or children's garment, the yarn-over buttonhole might be your best bet. It produces an especially small opening in the fabric. To create this buttonhole, knit two stitches together, followed by a yarn over. On the return row, work the yarn over as a stitch.

Yarn over between two knit stitches. Bring the yarn from the back of the work to the front between the two needles. Knit the next stitch, bringing the yarn to the back over the right needle as shown.

Tip: Not sure how many buttons you need? It's always best to have space for more. The smaller the gaps between buttons, the flatter and smoother your cardigan band will appear. It's also good to buy the buttons for your project before you start knitting so that you'll have an idea of the size, spacing, and number of buttonholes on the buttonhole band.

The goal is to space your buttonholes as evenly as possible. Accomplish this by placing markers on the button band for the first and last buttonholes. Measure the distance between them and place markers evenly for the remaining buttonholes.

Ensure your buttons and buttonholes line up in the end by following this easy tip: Count the number of rows between the lower edge and the first marker, between the first and second markers, and so on. Make a note of how many rows separate each marker, and then make your buttonholes on the corresponding rows of the buttonhole band.

Tip: Most patterns suggest that the button and buttonhole bands be worked separately and sewn on later. You can also work the front bands with the main piece on some styles. This easy method saves time and eliminates the need for extra seaming. This technique also allows you to space the buttonholes precisely along the edge of the sweater.

Button Up

When you are ready to sew on the buttons, you can use yarn (if it will pass through the button) or matching thread. With metal buttons, which may cut the thread, you may wish to use waxed dental floss. Double the thread and tie a knot on the end. Then slip your button onto the needle and thread. You can further secure the button with a square of fabric or felt at the back, which is especially desirable on garments like jackets that receive heavy wear.

Knotted thread has a tendency to pull through knit fabric. Lock it in place by inserting thread into the fabric on the right side and through the doubled thread. Clip knotted end.

Picking Up the Neck

When picking up stitches for a sloped edge (such as for a neck), take a little more care than for a straight edge. Much of this effort comes in the spacing. It's especially important that the stitches be picked up evenly when you are making a neckband, so the band will not flare out (too many stitches picked up) or pull in (too few stitches picked up).

Chapter five: A basic stitch sampler

Some people are content sticking with stockinette, but chances are, once you've grown CONFIDENT with the basics, you'll want to go BEYOND the garter, so to speak.

There are two ways to attain INTEREST in knitted fabrics—color and texture. The yarns you choose can have amazing results, but you already know that. At this point, you can add COLOR WORK and STITCH WORK to the equation for a beautiful outcome. This is when your project becomes a lot more interesting.

Add Some Texture

It's time to revisit ribbing. Remember when we alternated knits and purls within a row to create nice stretchy ribs? This stretchy quality makes ribbing the preferred stitch for sweater cuffs and hems. Ribbed fabrics are reversible, which makes ribbing perfect for scarves. In addition to several variations on the ribbing theme, there are myriad other easy ways of combining stitches to create texture in a knitted fabric, many of which simply involve alternating stitches within a row.

Ribbing

Most popular among ribbings are the ever-present k1, p1 and k2, p2 combinations, seen on sweaters everywhere. Actually, you can knit a ribbing in just about any combination of knits and purls. Here are some of our favorites:

Twisted K1, P1 (half twist)
An odd number of stitches
Row 1 (right side) **Knit one through the back loop, *purl one, knit one through the back loop; repeat from * to end.**
Row 2 **Purl one, *knit one, purl one; repeat from * to end.**
Repeat rows 1 and 2.

Twisted K1, P1 (full twist)

An odd number of stitches

Row 1 (right side) **Knit one through the back loop, *purl one, knit one through the back loop; repeat from * to end.**

Row 2 **Purl one through the back loop, *knit one, purl one through the back loop; repeat from * to end.**

Repeat rows 1 and 2.

K5, P2

Multiple of 7 stitches plus 2 extra

Row 1 (wrong side) **K2, *p5, k2; repeat from * to end.**

Row 2 **P2, *k5, p2; repeat from * to end.**

Repeat rows 1 and 2.

K2, P5

Knit two, purl five ribbing

Multiple of 7 stitches plus 2 extra

Row 1 (right side) **K2, *p5, k2; repeat from * to end.**

Row 2 **P2, *k5, p2; repeat from * to end.**

Repeat rows 1 and 2.

It might be some time before you are ready to reel yourself into an entire Irish fisherman's sweater, each one unique in its intricate texture. You'll be pleasantly surprised, however, to discover that some of the prettiest textured stitches are the easiest to knit. The beautiful seed stitch, for example, requires a simple knit one, purl one, and alternates on the next row with purl one, knit one (see below). How lovely would it be to create a patchwork blanket of swatches—made up of all the new stitches you are learning!

Seed Stitch
(over an even number of sts)
Row 1 (RS) ***K1, p1; rep from * to end.**
Row 2 ***P1, k1; rep from * to end.**
Rep rows 1 and 2.

Moss Stitch
(multiple of 2 sts plus 1)
Rows 1 and 3 (RS) **Knit.**
Row 2 **P1, *k1, p1; rep from * to end.**
Row 4 **K1, *p1; k1; rep from * to end.**
Rep rows 1–4.

Horizontal Dash Stitch

(multiple of 10 sts plus 6)

Row 1 (RS) P6, *k4, p6; rep from * to end.

Row 2 and all WS rows Purl.

Row 3 Knit.

Row 5 P1, *k4, p6; rep from *, end last rep p1.

Row 7 Knit.

Row 8 Purl.

Rep rows 1–8.

Basketweave

(multiple of 8 sts plus 5)

Row 1 (RS) Knit.

Row 2 K5, *p3, k5; rep from * to end.

Row 3 P5, *k3, p5; rep from * to end.

Row 4 Rep row 2.

Row 5 Knit.

Row 6 K1, *p3, k5; rep from *, end last rep k1.

Row 7 P1, *k3, p5; rep from *, end last rep p1.

Row 8 Rep row 6.

Rep rows 1–8.

Embossed Diamonds

(multiple of 10 sts plus 3)

Row 1 (RS) P1, k1, p1, *[k3, p1] twice, k1, p1; rep from * to end.

Row 2 P1, k1, *p3, k1, p1, k1, p3, k1; rep from *, end p1.

Row 3 K4, *[p1, k1] twice, p1, k5; rep from*, end last rep k4.

Row 4 P3, *[k1, p1] 3 times, k1, p3; rep from * to end.

Row 5 Rep row 3.

Row 6 Rep row 2.

Row 7 Rep row 1.

Row 8 P1, k1, p1, *k1, p5, [k1, p1] twice; rep from * to end.

Row 9 [P1, k1] twice, *p1, k3, [p1, k1] 3 times; rep from *, end last rep [p1,k1] twice, p1.

Row 10 Rep row 8.

Rep rows 1–10.

Color My World

"For me, it's all about color. Color is magic," relates Kaffe Fassett, a master color work knitter. Now in his sixties, Fassett is a knitter in his prime. He originally discovered yarn while visiting Scotland, and went on to learn to knit while on the train ride back to London. "Since then," he says, "I've painted with yarn."

The easiest method of changing colors is simply to knit horizontal stripes. All you need to do is change colors at the ends of rows, carrying the unused color along the edge of your knitting. This technique is a favorite among neophyte knitters who are eager to delve into the wonderful world of using multiple colors of yarns but are still timid about attempting anything too complicated. It's true enough that you could change colors countless times, and not run out of new shades, considering the myriad colors constantly available.

When you want to move on from stripes, remember that when dealing with color work, you must do whatever you can to keep your yarns from becoming twisted. With just two colors, it's easy—keep one color to your right and one to your left. It gets a little more complicated when you use several colors at the same time, but, we aren't ready to talk about that just yet.

Simply Fair Isle

Who hasn't seen a lovely Fair Isle sweater and wanted one for her very own? Such an ambitious project will have to wait a little while. Despite its intricate appearance, Fair Isle knitting usually calls for only two colors of yarn in each row (so you can hold one color in each hand) and no more than 5–7 consecutive stitches in any one color. Each color has a symbol, and patterns are clearly charted on graph paper. It's not as complicated as it may look.

Intarsia

Is it your heart's desire to adorn your bedroom with heart pillows, or maybe a special Halloween pumpkin sweater for your grandson? For isolated blocks or shapes, learning intarsia is necessary. As with Fair Isle, you'll be using two balls of yarn, but this time you can knit big shapes with the second color. This is also known as "picture knitting." After you've mastered this fun technique, you can create all kinds of cool things for friends and family.

Perfecting Pop-Ups

Raised stitches such as knots and popcorns seem to appeal to kids of all ages. This is a great way to add texture to children's and baby garments. When knitting a raised stitch, you'll be increasing several stitches in one stitch and knitting a little ball that sticks up on the surface of your knitting. Knots are made by forming little loops on the front of the knitting. Raised stitches can be placed randomly or in a regular pattern to create overall texture.

Peppercorn stitch
(multiple of 4 sts plus 3)
Peppercorn st: K next st, [sl st just knit back to LH needle and knit it again tbl] 3 times.
Row 1 (RS) **K3, *peppercorn st, k3; rep from * to end.**
Row 2 **Purl.**
Row 3 **K1, *peppercorn st, k3; rep from *, end last rep k1.**
Row 4 **Purl.**
Rep rows 1–4.

Bramble/blackberry stitch
(multiple of 4 sts)
Row 1 (RS) **Purl.**
Row 2 ***[K1, p1, k1] in same st, p3tog; rep from * to end.**
Row 3 **Purl.**
Row 4 ***P3tog, [k1, p1, k1] in same st; rep from * to end.**
Rep rows 1–4.

Dot-knot Stitch: Insert RH needle from front to back under horizontal strand between 1st and 2nd sts on LH needle, wrap yarn and draw through a loop loosely; insert RH needle between same sts above horizontal strand, draw through another loop loosely; bring yarn to front between needles and purl the first st on LH needle; with point of LH needle, pass the first loop over the 2nd loop and the purled st and off needle; pass the 2nd loop over the purled st and off needle.

Dot-knot stitch
(multiple of 6 sts plus 1)
Row 1 (RS) Knit.
Row 2 and all WS rows Purl.
Row 3 K3, *work dot-knot stitch, k5; rep from *, end last rep k3.
Row 5 Knit.
Row 7 *Work dot-knot st, k5; rep from *, end k1.
Row 8 Purl.
Rep rows 1–8.

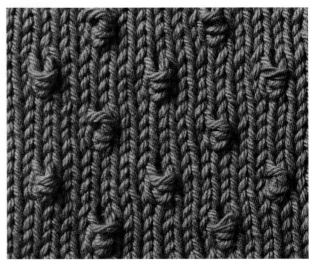

Hole-Y Knitting!

Think back to earlier in this book when we went over buttonholes. This same yarn-over technique can be used to make gorgeous lace! It's rare that you will have a reason to knit lingerie, but it's easy to learn how to knit simple eyelet trims and inserts once you become accustomed to having holes in your knitting. As with Fair Isle knitting, most openwork stitches are charted out—perfect for those of us with a short attention span!

Basic Openwork Stitches

Eyelet Rows
(multiple of 2 sts plus 2)
Rows 1, 5, 7, 9, 13 and 15 (RS) Knit.
Row 2 and all WS rows Purl.
Row 3 K1, *yo, SKP; rep from *, end k1.
Row 11 K1, *SKP, yo; rep from *, end k1.
Row 16 Knit.
Rep rows 1–16.

Open leaves
(multiple of 12 sts plus 1)

Row 1 (RS) K1, *k3, k2tog, yo, k1, yo, SKP, k4; rep from * to end.

Row 2 and all WS rows Purl.

Row 3 K1, *k2, k2tog, [k1, yo] twice, k1, SKP, k3; rep from * to end.

Row 5 K1, *k1, k2tog, k2, yo, k1, yo, k2, SKP, k2; rep from * to end.

Row 7 K1, *k2tog, k3, yo, k1, yo, k3, SKP, k1; rep from * to end.

Row 9 Knit.

Row 11 K1, *yo, SKP, k7, k2tog, yo, k1; rep from * to end.

Row 13 K1, *yo, k1, SKP, k5, k2tog, k1, yo, k1; rep from * to end.

Row 15 K1, *yo, k2, SKP, k3, k2tog, k2, yo, k1; rep from * to end.

Row 17 K1, *yo, k3, SKP, k1, k2tog, k3, yo, k1; rep from * to end.

Row 19 Knit.

Row 20 Purl.

Rep rows 1–20.

Chevron eyelets
(multiple of 9 sts)

Row 1 (RS) *K4, yo, SKP, k3; rep from * to end.

Row 2 and all WS rows Purl.

Row 3 *K2, k2tog, yo, k1, yo, SKP, k2; rep from * to end.

Row 5 *K1, k2tog, yo, k3, yo, SKP, k1; rep from * to end.

Row 7 *K2tog, yo, k5, yo, SKP; rep from * to end.

Row 8 Purl.

Rep rows 1–8.

Simple Vine

(multiple of 11 sts plus 1)

Row 1 (RS) **K2tog, *k5, yo, k1, yo, k2, sl 1, k2tog, psso; rep from *, end last rep ssk.**

Row 2 and all WS rows **Purl.**

Row 3 **K2tog, *k4, yo, k3, yo, k1, sl 1, k2tog, psso; rep from *, end last rep ssk.**

Row 5 **K2tog, *k3, yo, k5, yo, sl 1, k2tog, psso; rep from *, end last rep ssk.**

Row 7 **K2tog, *k2, yo, k1, yo, k5, sl 1, k2tog, psso; rep from *, end last rep ssk.**

Row 9 **K2tog, *k1, yo, k3, yo, k4, sl 1, k2tog, psso; rep from *, end last rep ssk.**

Row 11 **K2tog, *yo, k5, yo, k3, sl 1, k2tog, psso; rep from *, end last rep ssk.**

Row 12 **Rep row 2.**

Rep rows 1–12.

Basic Cable

This book would not be complete without some sort of introduction to cables. As with anything worthwhile, knitting involves practice, practice, practice. After all the work you've done, you are probably ready to give some basic cables a try. To make cables, you will need small, double-pointed needles called cable needles. Cable needles work as placeholders for stitches you need to come back to. By knitting "out of order," we can create an intriguing twisted effect. This concept can't truly be understood until you give it a try. Most cables are worked as knit stitches over a purl background, and many come with a chart. First test the waters with a mock cable that does not require a cable needle, then take the leap with a giant cable.

Simple Mock Cable
(multiple of 4 sts plus 2)
2-st right twist (RT) K2tog leaving both sts on needle; insert RH needle between 2 sts, and k first st again; then sl both sts from needle.
Row 1 P2, *k2, p2; rep from * to end.
Rows 2 and 4 K2, *p2, k2; rep from * to end.
Row 3 P2, *RT, p2; rep from * to end.
Rep rows 1–4.

Giant Cable

Right cable
(panel of 16 sts)
12-st right cable Sl 6 sts to cn and hold to back of work, k6, k6 from cn.
Rows 1 and 3 (RS) P2, k12, p2.
Row 2 and all WS rows K the knit sts and p the purl sts.
Row 5 P2, 12-st right cable, p2.
Row 7 Rep row 1.
Row 8 Rep row 2.
Rep rows 1–8.

Left cable
(panel of 16 sts)
12-st left cable Sl 6 sts to cn and hold to front of work, k6, k6 from cn.
Rows 1 and 3 (RS) P2, k12, p2.
Row 2 and all WS rows K the knit sts and p the purl sts.
Row 5 P2, 12-st left cable, p2.
Row 7 Rep row 1.
Row 8 Rep row 2.
Rep rows 1–8.

Chapter six: The knitting community

Ask knitters of any age why they LOVE to knit.
Aside from relaxation, many will say it's because it affords
them the OPPORTUNITY to be a part of a whole
community of PEOPLE with similiar interests.

Mary Colucci, an avid knitter "of a certain age" and the executive director of the Craft Yarn Council of America, concurs, "One of the biggest trends I've observed among knitters and crocheters is how much they enjoy the SOCIAL aspect of these crafts and getting together in formal and informal groups." When we enter middle age, this is especially CRUCIAL, as it is a time of life when loneliness is very common. The kids are growing up and leaving the house, and although we are proud of them, it's a stressful time. After all, our kids have been telling us for years to "get a life." With knitting, now we can. Aside from all that, even with your kids out of the house, your knitting—and the projects you create—can be a great way to stay in TOUCH and RECONNECT.

Teach the Children

Knitting is very much a contagious hobby. If you take the time to share your new interest with the public, pretty soon you will be asked to teach someone how to knit. In history, knitting knowledge was passed down from the older generation to the younger. In modern times, the warm picture of the white-haired granny sharing her wise old adages to her loving grandchildren is out of date. These are the days when it's cool to knit, and age is no longer a barrier. Very often, the teacher might be younger than the student, but still, the concept of passing on tradition is an important part of the bonding experience of knitting.

If your children or grandchildren are eager to learn to knit, Alison Ellen, author of *Hand Knitting: New Directions* (Crowood Press, 2002), believes "children can be taught to knit from the age of five or six." Ellen suggests keeping little ones on your lap as you teach them. For more than 75 years, knitting has been part of the K–4 curriculum at Waldorf Schools, based on the teachings of Austrian-born philosopher and social thinker Rudolf Steiner. In fact, kids attending Waldorf Schools or home-schooled in the Waldorf methods are taught knitting before they learn to read or do math. "When we teach a child to knit or make something useful by hand, we are then working on the spirit of the child," states Barbara Dewey in The Waldorf Handwork for Homeschoolers, K-4. "Activities of this kind, performed by the hands, lead to an enhancement of the faculty of judgment." If you think it's time to give it a try, here are some tips from the Craft Yarn Council:

- Keep it fun.
- Have a model of the project they will be making so they can see their progress.
- Select simple projects and use fun, bright colors.
- Keep lessons short to accommodate their short attention spans.
- Don't expect perfection, and praise them often.
- Showing is better then telling. Demonstrate the skill that you want them to do.

Lesson One: Make sure the television stays off. Grab some size 10 wooden needles and a couple skeins of good-quality worsted wool yarn, gather your patience, and hop a grandkid on your lap. You might want to do the cast-on row yourself. Then, remember this little rhyme to keep you both on track:

In through the front door
Around the back
Out through the window
And off jumps Jack.

If the person you are teaching is a teen or will be one soon, he or she already knows that knitting is now considered cool. It's possible that your teenage kids or grandkids have already been pressing their hip granny for tips. If you've recently felt like the teens in your life might be living on another planet, knitting can help you reconnect with them. Knitting can't actually turn back the clock (not that you'd ever want to be a teenager again), but it can be a fun and productive way to connect with an age group you were afraid you'd lost touch with. Imagine all the great fashion accessories you can knit together! A hint for those with teens at home: If you make two of each item, you're not as likely to have that pesky "borrowing" problem. Today's young people are under lots of pressure. Like us, they are using knitting for stress relief. So think of it not so much as teaching a domestic skill as helping teenagers develop a new coping mechanism.

Are You Certifiable?

It's possible you will discover you enjoy knitting so much that you want to make it into a career. Teaching crafts is a fun way to earn some extra money or provide community service. Knitting is more popular than ever, and consequently the need for teachers is greater than ever before. The Craft Yarn Council offers a three-level program taught by leading knitting and crochet teachers. All you need in order to apply are advanced beginner's skills and the enthusiasm to teach. The Craft Yarn Council also offers on-site workshops at New York's prestigious Fashion Institute of Technology, as well as correspondence courses where completed work is submitted by mail and reviewed by an instructor. Once you've completed the course and have the well-regarded credentials, you'll be able to teach at local craft stores and yarn shops all over the country. You may discover that you have a new career—one that has flexible hours and can go anywhere you go.

If you are interested in further knitting training, The Knitting Guild Association (TKGA) offers a master knitter program, which also has three levels of training. After you have mastered the top level, you'll be knitting multi-colored Aran sweaters, designing your own garments, and writing book reviews!

A Close-Knit Group

Over time, knitting has become known as a solitary activity. Actually, that's what some people like most about it. Ironically though, for those who feel lonely, the social aspects of knitting can have great healing value. Psychologists agree that the best way to cope with feelings of loneliness is to join a group of people with common interests. Knitting groups are perfect for this because you can work hard on your pattern while chatting and snacking with your friends. Fifty-year-old Maria Bowdich, a French teacher at a co-ed boarding school, noticed that many of the girls in her dorm had taken up knitting. She decided it was finally time to learn. "I was at a point in my life where I wanted to do something just for me," she says. She joined a local knitting group and discovered that, aside from having people to knit with, the group became a sort of emotional support system. "Knitting is a great neutralizer," adds Judith L. Swartz, knitting teacher, designer, and author of *Hip to Knit* (Interweave Press, 2002). "I've noticed that once people pick up their knitting needles in a class or club, they tend to drop all age and political differences."

If you are interested in finding a nearby knitting group, ask about it at the local library, recreation center, church, coffee house, yarn shop, or craft store. The Internet is also very useful. Visit websites such as www.meetup.com/knitting, which boasts 664 groups worldwide. Simply visit the site and type in your zip code to find a group of knitters near you. If you are the type that has a lot of angst to get off your chest, check out www.stitchnbitch.org, and look for a Stitch 'n Bitch group in your area.

If you can't find a group in your area, start one up yourself! The Craft Yarn Council has these suggestions:

- Decide how big you want your group to be and how often to meet.

- Consider the best location—members' homes, town meeting places (library, church, recreation center), or commercial venue (coffee shop or yarn store).
- Have everyone bring a completed project as a "show and tell" icebreaker. New knitters can bring a picture of something they want to make.
- Set a regular knitting time and some achievable goals.

For people who can't get around as much, there are plenty of chat rooms on the Internet that offer technical assistance, project ideas, and even pain management tips. A random visit to the website www.knittersreview.com/forum yields literally hundreds of suggestions on how to deal with knitter's elbow: "Prop arms up with pillows while knitting," "Use homeopathic arnica gel," "Take frequent breaks," "Acupuncture," "Get a massage," and so on. How can someone even dream of being isolated when there are thousands of people to talk to?

Guilds with a Conscience

Way back in history, knitting was solely the domain of men. The first knitting trade guild was started in Paris in 1527. If the concept of an all-male knitting group sounds appealing, no worries—you won't have to travel far to find a guild near you. How is a guild different from a club? By definition, guilds tend to be more structured than clubs and are usually organized under the banner of an organization like The Knitting Guild Association. Chicago's Windy City Knitting Guild is one of the country's largest, boasting almost 250 members. Member and past president Joyce Chan feels that the $20 annual membership fee is a small price to pay for the benefits it provides, which include a monthly newsletter, access to the group's own website, and the support of the city's huge knitting community. Mary Colucci adds, "The camaraderie these groups develop is often channeled into charity knitting programs, with people putting aside individual projects to knit and crochet for people in need." There are almost 200 guilds registered on The Knitting Guild Association's official website: www.tkga.com.

Mentoring

If you have reached the point where you are comfortable with your knitting and feel confident in your craft, you might want to join the Needle Arts Mentoring Program (NAMP), which goes into schools to teach kids how to knit. Improved hand-eye coordination and practice with problem solving are just two of the benefits knitting can have for kids. Students with attention deficit disorder especially have made visible progress with the program. See www.needleartsmentoring.org for more information.

Feeling Charitable?

At some point in your life, you've seen images of posters from World War I that proclaim "Uncle Sam wants YOU—to knit!" It all began when the sole woman on the Red Cross Central Commission at the start of the war realized that our boys on the front lines wouldn't survive the winter without sweaters, socks, mittens, and helmets. In response, the Red Cross sent out the word (and patterns) to its local chapters. By the war's end, the people at home had knit more than 24 million military garments! This Red Cross tradition continues today and has inspired countless other charities, including Afghans for Afghans, a program that sends handmade afghans, hats, vests, mittens, and socks to the besieged people of Afghanistan.

Many people start out knitting as a solitary pastime, only to discover it is the key to rejoining society. In your neighborhood, even worldwide, there are hundreds of organizations that help transform your newborn love into community service. "When one knits for others, known or unknown to them, the opportunity is presented to knit a bit of oneself into the piece," observes Candace Key on the blog *Knitty.com*.

Local hospitals often have programs where knitters can donate caps for preemies, knit bears for kids with cancer, or make shawls for the elderly in need. Other programs provide stuffed animals for kids in shelters (www.cubsforkids.com) and hats for the homeless (www.hats4thehomeless.org). For a comprehensive list of charities, visit www.interweave.com/knit/charities.

Got the Travel Bug?

An added bonus for the traveling knitter: Not only is knitting portable, but it actually can create its own traveling opportunities. In the British Isles, for example, the knitting tradition is booming. Joyce James Tours (www.joycejames-tours.com) offers trips to Scotland, Ireland, England, and Iceland that include visits with local craftspeople for travelers with an interest in fiber arts. (For those with partners whose interests tend more toward activities like golf, accommodations can be made!) Designer Jean Moss (www.jeanmoss.com) organizes tours in England and Wales that feature visits to the studios of well-known hand-knit designers, as well as side trips for spouses with other interests. For the real purists, famous Shetland wool producers Jamieson Wool Brokers run an annual Shetland Island Knitting Escape that tours these wool- (and sweater-) producing islands off the coast of Scotland (www.simplyscot-land.net). Arnhild Hellkas (www.arnhild.com) takes tour groups to Scandinavia and northern European countries with rich textile traditions. Closer to home, fiber-oriented holidays include Camp Stitches (www.knittinguniverse.com) and Meg Swansen's Knitting Camps and Retreats (www.schoolhousepress.com). All you need is yarn and your passport!

Essentially, knitting is a way of turning yarn into cloth. However, it should be clear to you by now that it represents so much more than that. It's multi-generational, unisex, international, creative, fashionable, therapeutic, sociable, and even charitable. But most importantly, knitting is fun!

Chapter seven: Easy patterns

As soon as you learn the knit stitch, you are
ready to start making your own garments.
Here are 18 patterns to try at home.

Yin scarf

A scarf is a great first project, giving you a chance to show off your new knitting skills. This first of a pair of scarves designed by Christie Furber lets you pick a color to suit your mood.

SCARF

Cast on 14 sts. Work even in garter st (knit every row) until piece measures 62"/157.5cm from beg. Bind off.

KNITTED MEASUREMENTS

• Approx 4" x 62"/10 x 157.5cm

MATERIALS

• 2 balls in #140 rose of *Lion Suede* by Lion Brand, 3oz/85g balls, each approx 122yd/110m (polyester)
• One pair size 9 (5.5mm) needles or size to obtain gauge

GAUGE

14 sts and 28 rows to 4"/10cm over garter st using size 9 (5.5mm) needles.
Take time to check gauge.

Yin and Yang scarf

If you're up to the challenge of a two-color project, make the Yin and Yang scarf, designed by Christie Furber.

Note When changing colors for yin and yang scarf, pick up new color from under dropped color to prevent holes.

SCARF

With A, cast on 12 sts, then with B, cast on 12 sts.

Row 1 (WS) With B, k12, with A, k12.

Row 2 With A, k12, with B, k12. Rep these 2 rows until piece measures 60"/152.5cm from beg. Bind off.

KNITTED MEASUREMENTS

Approx 7" x 60"/17.5 x 152.5cm

MATERIALS

• **1 ball each in #178 teal (A) and #153 ebony (B) of** *Lion Suede* **by Lion Brand, 3oz/85g balls, each approx 122yd/110m (polyester)**

• **One pair size 9 (5.5mm) needles or size to obtain gauge**

GAUGE

14 sts and 28 rows to 4"/10cm over garter st using size 9 (5.5mm) needles.

Take time to check gauge.

His and Hers hats

Knit flat with a back seam, these classic watch caps designed by Darlene Jackson work up fast in a super bulky wool blend. The crown decreases neatly disappear into the ever-narrowing ribbing.

RIB PATTERN

(multiple of 8 sts)

Row 1 (RS) *K4, p4; rep from * to end.

Rep row 1 for rib pat.

HAT

Cast on 58 (66) sts.

Next row (RS) K1 (selvage st), place st marker, work in rib pat across next 56 (64) sts, place st marker, k1 (selvage st). Keeping 1 st each side in garter st (k every row), cont to work rem sts in rib pat. Work even until piece measures 6"/15cm from beg, end with a WS row.

Crown shaping

Row 1 (RS) K1 (selvage st), *k1, k2tog, k1, p1, p2tog, p1; rep from *, end k1 (selvage st)—44 (50) sts.

Row 2 K1 (selvage st), *k3, p3; rep from *, end k1 (selvage st).

Row 3 K1 (selvage st), *k2tog, k1, p2tog, p1; rep from *, end k1 (selvage st)—30 (34) sts.

SIZES

Instructions are written for size Small/Medium. Changes for Medium/Large are in parentheses.

KNITTED MEASUREMENTS

Head circumference 21¾ (24¾)"/55 (63)cm

MATERIALS

• 1 ball in #180 evergreen (His) or 1 ball in #130 grass (Hers) of *Wool-Ease Chunky* by Lion Brand, 5oz/140g balls, each approx 153yd/140m (acrylic/wool)

• One pair size 11 (8mm) needles or size to obtain gauge

• Stitch markers

GAUGE

8 sts and 11 rows to 3"/7.5cm over rib pat using size 11 (8mm) needles.

Take time to check gauge.

Row 4 K1 (selvage st), *k2, p2; rep from *, end k1 (selvage st).

Row 5 K1 (selvage st), *k2, p2tog; rep from *, end k1 (selvage st)—23 (26) sts.

Row 6 K1 (selvage st), drop marker, *k1, p2tog; rep from *, end drop marker, k1 (selvage st)—16 (18) sts.

Row 7 [K2tog] 8 (9) times—8 (9) sts. Cut yarn leaving a long end. Thread tail in tapestry needle and weave through sts. Pull tight to gather, fasten off securely, then sew back seam.

Trellis shawl

Ann E. Smith's Trellis shawl (named for the elegant novelty yarn she chose) provides quick-knit glamour for all skill levels. No finishing required—bind off, put it on, and go.

Trellis shawl

Note A circular needle is used to accommodate the large number of stitches.

SHAWL

Cast on 225 sts. Do not join. Work back and forth in St st (knit one row, purl one row) until piece measures 18"/45.5cm from beg, end with a RS row. Bind off all sts knitwise.

KNITTED MEASUREMENTS

Approx 18" x 60"/45.5 x 152.5cm

MATERIALS

• 6 balls in #302 ocean of *Trellis* by Lion Brand, 1¾oz/50g balls, each approx 115yd/105m (nylon)
• Size 13 (9mm) circular needle, 36"/91.5cm long or size to obtain gauge

GAUGE

15 sts and 20 rows to 4"/10cm over St st using size 13 (9mm) needle.

Take time to check gauge.

Mohair poncho

Simple garter stitch is all you need to create Veronica Manno's cozy poncho. Sew up the panels, add a pretty ribbon, and you're good to go.

Note Poncho is made of two rectangular pieces which are sewn to each other leaving a neck opening (see assembly diagram).

PONCHO

(make 2 pieces)

Cast on 54 sts. Work even in garter st until piece measures 33"/84cm from beg. Bind off.

FINISHING

Referring to assembly diagram, use yarn to sew cast-on edge of first piece to left-hand edge of second piece, matching points A and B. Sew bound-off edge of second piece to right-hand edge of first piece matching points C and D. Using yarn, sew a gathering thread along A/B seam. Pull to gather; fasten off securely. Tie ribbon into a bow. Sew bow in place using sewing thread as pictured.

SIZES

Instructions are written for one size.

KNITTED MEASUREMENTS

Each piece measures approx 18" x 33"/45.5 x 84cm

MATERIALS

• 4 balls in #201 rain forest of *Moonlight Mohair* by Lion Brand, 1¾oz/50g balls, each approx 82yd/75m (mohair/acrylic/cotton/polyester metallic blend)

• One pair size 11 (8mm) needles or size to obtain gauge

• 32"/81cm length of 1½"/38mm-wide ribbon

• Matching sewing thread

• Sewing needle

GAUGE

12 sts and 20 rows to 4"/10cm over garter st using size 11 (8mm) needles.

Take time to check gauge.

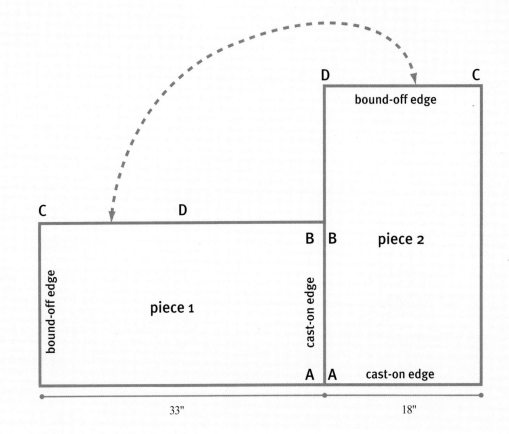

Baby blanket

Weave your best wishes for baby into this lush, cashmere blend blanket, designed by Margarita Mejia. The classic basketweave pattern is bordered on all sides by pretty seed stitch, which forms a self-finished edge.

SEED STITCH

(multiple of 2 sts)

Row 1 (RS) *K1, p1; rep from * to end.

Row 2 K the purl sts and p the knit sts.

Rep row 2 for seed st.

BASKETWEAVE PATTERN

(multiple of 8 sts plus 2)

Row 1 (WS) Purl.

Row 2 K2, *p6, k2; rep from * to end.

Row 3 P2, *k6, p2; rep from * to end.

Row 4 Rep row 2.

Row 5 Purl.

Row 6 P4, *k2, p6; rep from *, end k2, p4.

Row 7 K4, *p2, k6; rep from *, end p2, k4.

Row 8 Rep row 6.

Rep rows 1–8 for basketweave pat.

KNITTED MEASUREMENTS

Approx 24½" x 27 ½"/ 62 x 70cm

MATERIALS

• **7 balls in #101 light pink of *Lion Cashmere Blend* by Lion Brand, 1½oz/43g balls, each approx 84yd/77m (wool/nylon/cashmere)**

• **One pair size 8 (5mm) needles or size to obtain gauge**

• **Stitch markers**

GAUGE

19 sts and 32 rows to 4"/10cm over basketweave pat using size 8 (5mm) needles.

Take time to check gauge.

BLANKET

Beg at bottom border, cast on 116 sts. Do not join. Work back and forth in seed st for 2"/5cm.

Beg pats

Next row (WS) Work in seed st across first 9 sts, place st marker, work row 1 of basketweave pat across next 98 sts, place st marker, work in seed st across last 9 sts. Keeping 9 sts each side in seed st for side borders, work center 98 sts in basketweave pat and work even until piece measures 25½"/64.5cm from beg, end with row 5.

Next row (RS) Work in seed st across all sts dropping markers. Cont in seed st until top border measures 2"/5cm. Bind off in seed st.

Chevron afghan

This afghan will provide relaxation during and after its creation. Master the easy chevron pattern, and your knitting will develop a soothing rhythm. Finish the afghan and curl up with it for a well-deserved nap. Designed by Margarita Mejia.

Approx 42" x 57"/106.5 x 144.5cm

MATERIALS

• **1 ball each in #378 olive (A), #377 harvest (B), and #380 fawn (K) of** *Homespun* **by Lion Brand, 6oz/170g balls, each approx 185yd/167m (acrylic/polyester)**
• **1 ball each in #124 camel (C) and #173 grass green (G) of** *Jiffy* **by Lion Brand, 3oz/85g balls, each approx 135yd/123m (acrylic)**
• **1 ball each in #273 spring desert (F) and #275 autumn trails (L) of** *Landscapes* **by Lion Brand, 1¾oz/50g balls, each approx 55yd/50m (wool/acrylic)**
• **1 ball each in #201 rain forest (D) and #203 safari (J) of** *Moonlight Mohair* **by Lion Brand, 1¾oz/50g balls, each approx 82yd/75m (mohair/acrylic/cotton/poly-ester metallic blend)**

Chevron afghan

NOTE A circular needle is used to accommodate the large number of stitches.

CHEVRON PATTERN

(multiple of 13 sts plus 2)

Row 1 (RS) Purl.

Row 2 Knit.

Row 3 K2, *yo, k4, SK2P, k4, yo, k2; rep from * to end.

Row 4 Purl.

Row 5 Rep row 3.

Row 6 Purl.

Row 7 Rep row 3.

Row 8 Purl.

Row 9 Rep row 3.

Row 10 Purl.

Rep rows 1–10 for chevron pat.

AFGHAN

With A, cast on 123 sts. Do not join.

Next row (RS) K2, place st marker, p center 119 sts, place st marker, k2.

Next row Knit. Keeping 2 sts each side in garter st (k every row) for side borders, cont in chevron pat and stripe sequence on center 19 sts as folls: Work 10 rows each A, B, C, D, E, F, G, H, I, J, K, L, M, H, C, D, F, G, K, and B. Using B, work rows 1 and 2 twice more. Bind off.

• 1 ball in #194 lime (H) of *Lion Bouclé* by Lion Brand, 2½oz/70g balls, each approx 57yd/52m (acrylic/mohair/nylon)

• 1 ball each in #125 mocha (E) and #132 olive (M) of *Lion Suede* by Lion Brand, 3oz/85g balls, each approx 122yd/110m (polyester)

• 1 ball in #203 orchard print (I) of *Lion Suede Print* by Lion Brand, 3oz/85g balls, each approx 111yd/100m (polyester)

• Size 11 (8mm) circular needle, 36"/91.5cm long or size to obtain gauge

• Stitch markers

GAUGE

12 sts and 14 rows to 4"/10cm over pat st using a size 11 (8mm) needle.

Take time to check gauge.

Tank top

This simple tank design is a perfect fit for the young—or the young at heart. The vibrant multi-colored ribbon yarn makes Charlotte Parry's design a pleasure to knit and to wear.

K2, P2 RIB

(multiple of 4 sts plus 2)

Row 1 (RS) K2, *p2, k2; rep from * to end.

Row 2 P2, *k2, p2; rep from * to end.

Rep rows 1 and 2 for k2, p2 rib.

BACK

With smaller needles, cast on 54 (58, 62, 66, 74) sts. Work in k2, p2 rib for 1"/2.5cm, inc 0 (0, 2, 2, 0) sts evenly spaced across last row and end with a WS row—54 (58, 64, 68, 74) sts. Change to larger needles and work in St st until piece measures 11 (11, 11½, 12, 12½)"/28 (28, 29, 30.5, 31.5)cm from beg, end with a WS row.

Armhole shaping

Bind off 3 (3, 4, 4, 5) sts at beg of next 2 rows–48 (52, 56, 60, 64) sts.

Next (dec) row (RS) K1, SKP, k to last 3 sts, k2tog, k1. Purl next row. Rep last 2 rows 2 (3, 4, 5, 5) times more—42 (44, 46, 48, 52) sts. Work even until armhole measures 6½ (6½, 7, 7, 7½)"/16.5 (16.5, 17.5, 17.5, 19)cm, end with a WS row.

SIZES

Instructions are written for size X-Small. Changes for Small, Medium, Large, and X-Large are in parentheses.

KNITTED MEASUREMENTS

• Bust 33 (36, 39, 42, 45)"/84 (91.5, 99, 106.5, 114.5)cm

• Length 19½ (19½, 20½, 21, 22)"/49.5 (49.5, 52, 53.5, 56)cm

MATERIALS

• 4 (5, 5, 6 7) balls in #208 copper penny of *Incredible* by Lion Brand, 1¾oz/50g balls, each approx 110yd/100m (nylon)

• One pair each sizes 11 and 13 (8 and 9mm) needles or size to obtain gauge

GAUGE

13 sts and 14 rows to 4"/10cm over St st using larger needles. Take time to check gauge.

Neck shaping

Next row (RS) Work 16 (17, 17, 18, 19) sts, join a 2nd ball of yarn and bind off center 10 (10, 12, 12, 14) sts, work to end. Working both sides at once, dec 1 st at each neck edge every row 4 times—12 (13, 13, 14, 15) sts each side. Work even until armhole measures 8½ (8½, 9, 9, 9½)"/21.5 (21.5, 23, 23, 24)cm. Bind off sts each side for shoulders.

FRONT

Work as for back until armhole measures 4½ (4½, 5, 5, 5½)"/11.5 (11.5, 12.5, 12.5, 14)cm, end with a WS row.

Neck shaping

Next row (RS) Work 15 (16, 16, 17, 18) sts, join a 2nd ball of yarn and bind off center 12 (12, 14, 14, 16) sts, work to end. Working both sides at once, dec 1 st at each neck edge every other row 3 times—12 (13, 13, 14, 15) sts each side. Work even until piece measures same as back to shoulders. Bind off rem sts each side for shoulders.

FINISHING

Sew shoulder and side seams.

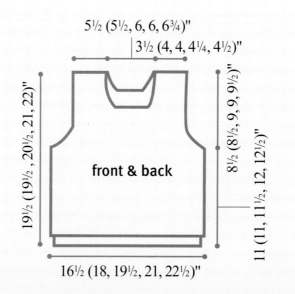

5½ (5½, 6, 6, 6¾)"

3½ (4, 4, 4¼, 4½)"

19½ (19½ , 20½ , 21, 22)"

8½ (8½, 9, 9, 9½)"

front & back

11 (11, 11½, 12, 12½)"

16½ (18, 19½, 21, 22½)"

Easy pullover

Susan Haviland's pullover makes a great "first sweater" project. Minimal shaping and chunky yarn will have you knitting it up in no time.

BACK

Cast on 30 (32, 35, 38) sts. Work even in St st until piece measures 8"/20.5cm from beg, end with a WS row.

Inc row (RS) K2, M1, k to last 2 sts, M1, k2—32 (34, 37, 40) sts. Work even until piece measures 14"/35.5cm from beg, end with a WS row.

Armhole shaping

Bind off 2 (2, 2, 3) sts at beg of next 2 rows—28 (30, 33, 34) sts.
Dec row (RS) K1, k2tog, k to last 3 sts, ssk, k1—26 (28, 31, 32) sts. Purl next row. Rep last 2 rows 2 (2, 3, 3) times more—22 (24, 25, 26) sts. Work even until armhole measures 7 (7½, 8, 9)"/17.5 (19, 20.5, 23)cm, end with a RS row.

Neck and shoulder shaping

Next row (WS) P 6 (7, 7, 7) sts, join another ball of yarn and bind off 10 (10, 11, 12) sts for neck, p to end.
Next row (RS) With first ball of yarn, bind off first 2 (3, 3, 3) sts, k to last 3 sts, ssk, k1, with second ball of yarn, k1, k2tog, k to end. Working both sides at once, bind off 2 (3, 3, 3) sts at beg of next row once, then 3 sts at beg of next 2 rows once.

SIZES

Instructions are written for size Small. Changes for Medium, Large, and X-Large are in parentheses.

KNITTED MEASUREMENTS

Bust 35 (39, 43, 47)"/89 (99, 109, 119)cm

Length 22½ (23, 23½, 24½)"/57 (58.5, 59.5, 62) cm

Upper arm 13 (14, 15,16)"/33 (35.5, 38, 40.5) cm

MATERIALS

• 5 (6, 7, 8) balls in #273 spring desert of *Landscapes* by Lion Brand, 1¾oz/50g balls, each approx 55yd/50m (wool/acrylic)
• One pair size 17 (12.75mm) needles or size to obtain gauge

GAUGE

7 sts and 12 rows = 4"/10cm using size 17 (12.75mm) needle. Take time to check gauge.

FRONT

Work as for back.

SLEEVES

Cast on 13 (13, 15, 15) sts. Work even in St st for 4 rows.

Inc row (RS) K2, M1, k to last 2 sts, M1, k2—15 (15, 17, 17) sts. Rep inc row every 6th row 4 (5, 5, 6) times more—23 (25, 27, 29) sts. Work even until piece measures 18"/45.5cm from beg, end with a WS row.

Cap shaping

Bind off 2 (2, 2, 3) sts at beg of next 2 rows—19 (21, 23, 23) sts.

Dec row (RS) K2, k2tog, k to last 4 sts, ssk, k2—17 (19, 21, 21) sts. Purl next row. Rep last 2 rows twice more—13 (15, 17, 17) sts. Work even for 2 (2, 4, 6) rows. Rep dec row on next row, then every other row 1 (2, 2, 2) times more, end with a WS row—9 (9, 11, 11) sts. Bind off 2 sts at beg of next 2 rows. Bind off rem 5 (5, 7, 7) sts.

FINISHING

Lightly block pieces to measurements. Sew shoulder seams. Set in sleeves. Sew side and sleeve seams.

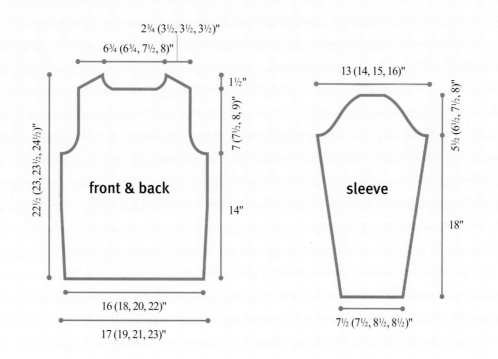

front & back

2¾ (3½, 3½, 3½)"

6¾ (6¾, 7½, 8)"

1½"

7 (7½, 8, 9)"

22½ (23, 23½, 24½)"

14"

16 (18, 20, 22)"

17 (19, 21, 23)"

sleeve

13 (14, 15, 16)"

5½ (6½, 7½, 8)"

18"

7½ (7½, 8½, 8½)"

Instructions are written for size
Small. Changes for Medium,
Large, X-Large, and XX-Large
are in parentheses.

KNITTED MEASUREMENTS

• Bust 37 (39, 41½, 44, 46)"/94 (99,
105.5, 111.5, 117)cm
• Length 22 1/2 (23, 23½, 24¼,
23¾)"/57 (58.5, 59.5, 61.5, 63)cm
• Upper arm 13 (14, 15, 16,
17)"/33 (35.5, 38, 40.5, 43)cm

MATERIALS

• 4 (4, 5, 5, 6) balls in #124 mocha
of *Microspun* by Lion Brand,
2½oz/70g balls, each approx
168yd/154m (microfiber acrylic)
• One pair size 11 (8mm) needles or size to obtain gauge
• Stitch markers

GAUGE

14 sts and 16 rows to 4"/10cm
over St st using size 11 (8mm)
needles.
Take time to check gauge.

Gossamer pullover

This easy-to-wear raglan pullover gives you the
opportunity to use your shaping skills. And you'll
have lots of practice, since the front and back pieces
are identical! Designed by Elena Malo.

BACK

Cast on 65 (69, 73, 77, 81) sts. Knit next 2 rows. Cont in St st until
piece measures 2"/5cm from beg, end with a WS row.

Dec row (RS) K1, ssk, k to last 3 sts, k2tog, k1. Rep dec row every
8th row once more—61 (65, 69, 73, 77) sts. Work even until piece
measures 11"/28cm from beg, end with a WS row.

Inc row (RS) K1, M1, k to last st, M1, k1. Rep inc row every 8th
row once more—65 (69, 73, 77, 81) sts. Work even until piece
measures 14"/35.5cm from beg, end with a WS row.

Raglan armhole shaping

Bind off 3 (3, 4, 4, 4) sts at beg of next 2 rows—59 (63, 65, 69,
73) sts.

Dec row (RS) K1, ssk, k to last 3 sts, k2tog, k1. Rep dec row every
other row 8 (9, 10, 11, 12) times more, then every 4th row 3 times,
end with a WS row—35 (37, 37, 39, 41) sts. Knit next 2 rows. Bind
off all sts knitwise.

FRONT

Work as for back.

SLEEVES

Cast on 33 (33, 35, 35, 37) sts. Knit next 2 rows. Cont in St st until piece measures 1½"/4cm from beg, end with a WS row.

Inc row (RS) K1, M1, k to last st, M1, k1. Rep inc row every 12th (8th, 8th, 6th, 6th) row 5 (7, 8, 10, 10) times more—45 (49, 53, 57, 59) sts. Work even until piece measures 17 (17, 18, 18, 18)"/43 (43, 45.5, 45.5, 45.5)cm from beg, end with a WS row.

Cap shaping

Bind off 3 (3, 4, 4, 4) sts at beg of next 2 rows—39 (43, 45, 49, 51) sts.

Dec row 1 (RS) K1, ssk, k to last 3 sts, k2tog, k1. Rep dec row every other row 11 (12, 13, 14, 15) times more, end with a RS row—15 (17, 17, 19, 19) sts.

Next row (WS) P 7 (8, 8, 9, 9), pm, p1, pm, p 7 (8, 8, 9, 9).

Dec row 2 (RS) K1, ssk, k to 2 sts before first marker, ssk, k1, k2tog, k to last 3 sts, k2tog, k1. Purl next row. Rep last 2 rows twice more dropping markers on last row and end with a WS row—3 (5, 5, 7, 7) sts.

For size Small only

Knit next 2 rows. Bind off all sts knitwise.

For sizes Medium and Large only:

Next row (RS) K1, SK2P, k1—3 sts. Knit next row. Bind off all sts knitwise.

For sizes X-Large and XX-Large only:

Next row (RS) K1, ssk, k1, k2tog, k1—5 sts. Knit next row. Bind off all sts knitwise.

FINISHING

Block pieces to measurements. Sew raglan sleeve caps to raglan armholes. Sew side and sleeve seams.

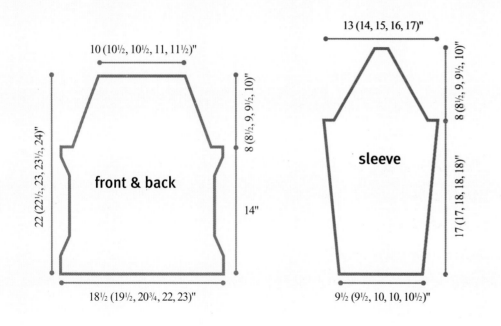

10 (10½, 10½, 11, 11½)"

13 (14, 15, 16, 17)"

8 (8½, 9, 9½, 10)"

8 (8½, 9, 9½, 10)"

front & back

sleeve

22 (22½, 23, 23½, 24)"

17 (17, 18, 18, 18)"

14"

18½ (19½, 20¾, 22, 23)"

9½ (9½, 10, 10, 10½)"

Instructions are written for size Small. Changes for Medium, Large, X-Large, and XX-Large are in parentheses.

KNITTED MEASUREMENTS

• Bust 36 (38, 41, 43, 45)"/91.5 (96.5, 104, 109, 114.5)cm

• Length 22½ (23½, 24½, 25½, 26½)"/57 (59.5, 62, 65, 67.5)cm

• Upper arm 13 (14, 15, 16, 17)"/33 (35.5, 38, 40.5, 43)cm

MATERIALS

• 4 (4, 5, 6, 6) balls in #362 quartz of *Homespun* by Lion Brand, 6oz/170g balls, each approx 185yd/167m (acrylic/polyester)

• One pair size 10½ (6.5mm) needles or size to obtain gauge

• Stitch markers

GAUGE

12 sts and 16 rows to 4"/10cm over St st using size 10½ (6.5mm) needles.

Take time to check gauge.

Boatneck pullover

Made for comfort and speed, this pullover designed by Elena Malo is quick to knit and extra comfy to wear in a soft, bulky-weight bouclé yarn.

BACK

Cast on 54 (58, 62, 64, 68) sts. Cont in St st for 2"/5cm, end with a WS row.

Dec row (RS) K1, ssk, k to last 3 sts, k2tog, k1. Rep dec row every 6th row twice more—48 (52, 56, 58, 62) sts. Work even until piece measures 10"/25.5cm from beg, end with a WS row.

Inc row (RS) K1, M1, k to last st, M1, k1. Rep inc row every 6th row twice more—54 (58, 62, 64, 68) sts. Work even until piece measures 15"/38cm from beg, end with a WS row.

Raglan armhole shaping

Bind off 3 sts at beg of next 2 rows—48 (52, 56, 58, 62) sts.

Dec row (RS) K1, ssk, k to last 3 sts, k2tog, k1. Rep dec row every 4th row 7 (8, 9, 10, 11) times more—32 (34, 36, 36, 38) sts. Bind off.

FRONT

Work as for back.

SLEEVES

Cast on 27 (29, 29, 31, 31) sts. Cont in St st for 1½"/4cm, end with a WS row.

Inc row (RS) K1, M1, k to last st, M1, k1. Rep inc row every 12th (10th, 8th, 8th, 6th) row 5 (6, 7, 8, 9) times more—39 (43, 45, 49, 51) sts. Work even until piece measures 18"/45.5cm from beg, end with a WS row.

Cap shaping

Bind off 3 sts at beg of next 2 rows—33 (37, 39, 43, 45) sts.

Dec row 1 (RS) K1, ssk, k to last 3 sts, k2tog, k1. Rep dec row every 4th row 3 (4, 5, 6, 7) times more, end with a RS row—25 (27, 27, 29, 29) sts.

Next row (WS) P 11 (12, 12, 13, 13), pm, p3, pm, p 11 (12, 12, 13, 13).

Dec row 2 (RS) K1, ssk, k to 2 sts before first marker, ssk, k3, k2tog, k to last 3 sts, k2tog, k1. Purl next row.

Dec row 3 (RS) K to 2 sts before first marker, ssk, k3, k2tog, k to end. Purl next row. Rep last 4 rows twice more dropping markers on last row and end with a WS row—7 (9, 9, 11, 11) sts.

For size Small only:

Next row (RS) K1, ssk, k1, k2tog, k1—5 sts. Purl next row. Bind off.

For sizes Medium and Large only:

Next row (RS) K1, ssk, SK2P, k2tog, k1—5 sts. Purl next row. Bind off.

For sizes X-Large and XX-Large only

Next row (RS) K1, SK2P, k3, k3tog, k1—7 sts. Purl next row. Bind off.

FINISHING

Block pieces to measurements. Sew raglan sleeve caps to raglan armholes. Sew side and sleeve seams.

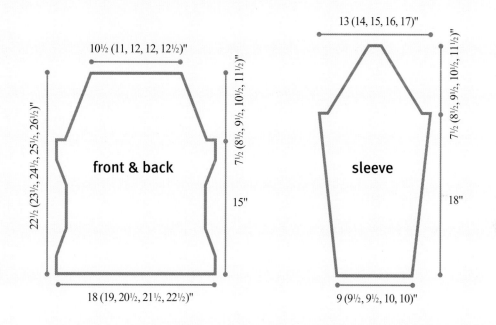

Moonlight Mohair jacket

Reverse stockinette stitch adds interest and texture to this elegant cardigan by Mari Lynn Patrick. Simple crochet edging adds a decorative element and keeps the borders from rolling.

BACK

Cast on 54 (56, 60, 66, 72) sts. Cont in reverse St st (purl 1 row, knit 1 row, with purl as RS) and work even until piece measures 4"/10cm from beg, end with a WS row. Dec 1 st each side on next row, then every 14th row once more—50 (52, 56, 62, 68) sts. Work even until piece measures 14"/35.5cm from beg, end with a WS row.

Armhole shaping

Bind off 3 sts at beg of next 2 rows, then 2 (2, 2, 3, 3) sts at beg of next 2 rows. Dec 1 st each side on next row, then every other row 1 (1, 2, 2, 3) times more—36 (38, 40, 44, 48) sts. Work even until armhole measures 7½ (8, 8½, 9, 9½)"/19 (20.5, 21.5, 23, 24)cm, end with a RS row.

Shoulder and neck shaping

Next row (WS) K 13 (14, 14, 16, 17), join another ball of yarn and bind off center 10 (10, 12, 12, 14) sts for back neck, k to end. Working both sides at once, bind off 4 (3, 3, 5, 4) sts at beg of next 2 rows, then 3 (4, 4, 4, 5) sts at beg of next 4 rows. AT THE SAME TIME, bind off 3 sts from each neck edge once.

SIZES

Instructions are written for size Small. Changes for Medium, Large, X-Large, and XX-Large are in parentheses.

KNITTED MEASUREMENTS

• Bust (closed) 36 (38, 41, 45, 49)"/91.5 (96.5, 104, 114.5, 124.5)cm
• Length 23 (23½, 24, 24½, 25)"/58.5 (59.5, 61, 62, 63.5)cm
• Upper arm 13 (14, 15, 16, 17)"/33 (35.5, 38, 40.5, 43)cm

MATERIALS

• 8 (8, 9, 10, 11) balls in #208 arctic circle of *Moonlight Mohair* by Lion Brand, 1¾oz/50g balls, each approx 82yd/75m (mohair/acrylic/cotton/poly-ester metallic blend)
• One pair size 13 (9mm) needles or size to obtain gauge
• Size J/10 (6mm) crochet hook

GAUGE

11 sts and 18 rows to 4"/10cm over pat st using size 13 (9mm) needles.
Take time to check gauge.

LEFT FRONT

Cast on 32 (33, 35, 38, 41) sts. Cont in reverse St st and work even until piece measures 4"/10cm from beg, end with a WS row. Dec 1 st at beg of next row (side edge) on next row, then every 14th row once more—30 (31, 33, 36, 39) sts. Work even until piece measures 14"/35.5cm from beg, end with a WS row.

Armhole shaping

Bind off 3 sts at beg of next row, then 2 (2, 2, 3, 3) sts at same edge once. Knit next row. Dec 1 st at armhole edge on next row, then at same edge every other row 1 (1, 2, 2, 3) times more—23 (24, 25, 27, 29) sts. Work even until armhole measures 4½ (5, 5½, 6, 6½)"/11.5 (12.5, 14, 15, 16.5)cm, end with a RS row.

Neck shaping

Next row (WS) Bind off 5 (5, 6, 6, 7) sts, k to end. Cont to bind off 2 sts from neck edge 4 times—10 (11, 11, 13, 14) sts. Work even until armhole measures same as back to shoulder, end with a WS row.

Shoulder shaping

Bind off 4 (3, 3, 5, 4) sts from armhole edge once, then 3 (4, 4, 4, 5) sts twice.

RIGHT FRONT

Work as for left front, reversing all shaping.

SLEEVES

Cast on 28 (28, 28, 30, 30) sts. Cont in reverse St st and work even for 2"/5cm, end with a WS row. Inc 1 st each side on next row, then every 14th (12th, 8th, 8th, 6th) row 3 (4, 6, 6, 7) times more—36 (38, 42, 44, 46) sts. Work even until piece measures 17½"/44.5cm from beg, end with a WS row.

Cap shaping

Bind off 3 sts at beg of next 2 rows. Dec 1 st each side on next row, then every other row 6 (7, 8, 9, 10) times more, then bind off 2 sts at beg of next 4 rows. Bind off rem 8 (8, 10, 10, 10) sts.

FINISHING

Lightly block pieces to measurements. Sew shoulder seams. Set in sleeves. Sew side and sleeve seams. Fold each front edge 1"/2.5cm to WS and tack in place.

Front and neck edging

With crochet hook and RS facing, join yarn with a sl st in bottom edge of left front.

Row 1 Ch 1, working from left to right and making sure that work lies flat, work in reverse sc as folls: Sc on first row, ch 1, skip next row, *sc in next row (or st), ch 1, skip next row (or st); rep from * to bottom edge of right front, end sc in last row. Fasten off.

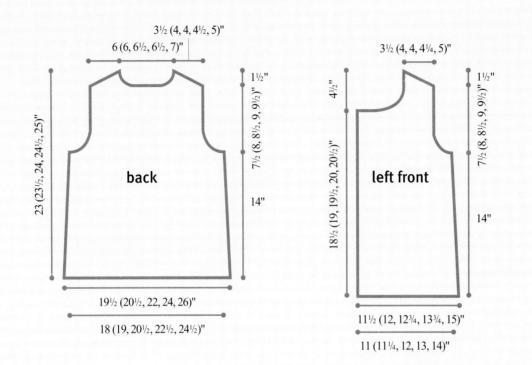

3½ (4, 4, 4½, 5)"

6 (6, 6½, 6½, 7)"

1½"

7½ (8, 8½, 9, 9½)"

14"

23 (23½, 24, 24½, 25)"

back

19½ (20½, 22, 24, 26)"

18 (19, 20½, 22½, 24½)"

3½ (4, 4, 4¼, 5)"

4½"

1½"

7½ (8, 8½, 9, 9½)"

14"

18½ (19, 19½, 20, 20½)"

left front

11½ (12, 12¾, 13¾, 15)"

11 (11¼, 12, 13, 14)"

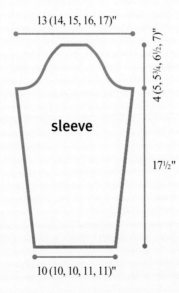

13 (14, 15, 16, 17)"

4 (5, 5¾, 6½, 7)"

sleeve

17½"

10 (10, 10, 11, 11)"

Baby booties

These far-from-standard booties are knit back and forth on straight needles starting at the center bottom sole, shaping the instep, and ending with a furry cuff. The resulting piece of knitting is folded and seamed from toe to cuff to create a perfect and stylish bootie for baby. Designed by Jean Guirguis.

One size fits 6–12 months.

KNITTED MEASUREMENTS

Sole measures approx 4"/10cm

long

MATERIALS

Version 1

• 1 ball in #153 black (MC) of

Lion Cashmere Blend by Lion

Brand, 1½oz/40g balls, each

approx 84yd/71m

(wool/nylon/cashmere)

• 1 ball in #100 white (CC) of

Fun Fur by Lion Brand, 1¾oz/50g

balls, each approx 60yd/54m

(polyester)

• One pair size 5 (3.75mm) nee-

dles or size to obtain gauge

• 1yd/1m of ¼"/6mm-wide white

and black polka dot satin ribbon

Baby booties

K1, P1 RIB

(multiple of 2 sts plus 1)

Row 1 (RS) K1, *p1, k1; rep from * to end.

Row 2 P1, *k1, p1; rep from * to end.

Rep rows 1and 2 for k1, p1 rib.

BOOTIES

Beg at center bottom of sole. With MC, cast on 28 sts.

Row 1 (RS) K2, M1, k10, [M1, k1] 4 times, k10, M1, k2—34 sts.

Row 2 Knit.

Row 3 K2, M1, k13, [M1, k1] 4 times, k13, M1, k2—40 sts.

Row 4 Knit.

Row 5 K2, M1, k16, [M1, k1] 4 times, k16, M1, k2—46 sts. Cont to work in garter st (k every row) until piece measures 1½"/4cm from beg, end with a WS row.

Instep shaping

Row 1 (RS) K19, k2tog, k8, turn (leave rem 17 sts unworked).

Row 2 Hold yarn to back of work, sl 1 as to purl, k8, k2tog, turn (leave rem 17 sts unworked).

Rows 3–6 Rep row 2, 4 times more. When row 6 is completed, you should have 15 unworked sts at each end.

Row 7 Yarn to front of work, sl 1 as to purl, k8, k2tog, turn (leave rem 14 sts unworked).

Row 8 Yarn to back of work, sl 1 as to purl, k8, k2tog, turn (leave rem 14 sts unworked).

Rows 9–16 Rep rows 7 and 8, 4 times more having one less unworked st at end of each row. When row 16 is completed, do not turn, knit across rem 10 unworked sts—30 sts on needle.

Cuff

Eyelet row (RS) K1, *yo, k2tog; rep from *, end yo, k1—31 sts.

Next row Knit. Change to CC and work even in k1, p1 rib for 2"/5cm. Bind off all sts.

FINISHING

For each bootie, sew cast-on edge of sole tog, then sew back seam. For version 1, cut ribbon in half, then weave each length through eyelets around cuff. Tie each into bows, then trim off excess ribbon at an angle.

MATERIALS

Version 2

• 1 ball in #101 light pink (MC) of *Lion Cashmere Blend* by Lion Brand, 1½oz/40g balls, each approx 84yd/71m (wool/nylon/cashmere)

• 1 ball in #213 fireworks (CC) of *Fun Fur Prints* by Lion Brand, 1½oz/40g balls, each approx 57yd/52m (polyester)

• One pair size 5 (3.75mm) needles or size to obtain gauge

GAUGE

20 sts and 28 rows to 4"/10cm over garter st using size 5 (3.75mm) needles.

Take time to check gauge.

Shawl Collar cardigan

Garter stitch and gentle shaping make for easy finishing of this design by Mari Lynn Patrick. A three-needle bind-off completes the collar join at the back neck edge.

BACK

Cast on 55 (59, 65, 69) sts. Cont in garter st and work even until piece measures 15½"/39.5cm from beg, end with a WS row.

Armhole shaping

Bind off 3 (3, 4, 4) sts at beg of next 2 rows. Dec 1 st each side on next row, then every other row 1 (2, 3, 3) times more—45 (47, 49, 53) sts. Work even until armhole measures 8 (8½, 9, 9½)"/20.5 (21.5, 23, 24)cm, end with a WS row.

Shoulder shaping

Bind off 4 (5, 5, 6) sts at beg of next 4 rows, then 5 (4, 5, 5) sts at beg of next 2 rows. Bind off rem 19 sts for back neck.

LEFT FRONT

Cast on 30 (32, 35, 37) sts. Cont in garter st and work even until piece measures 15½"/39.5cm from beg, end with a WS row.

Armhole and shawl collar shaping

Note Read through entire shaping directions before beg.

Next row (RS) Bind off 3 (3, 4, 4) sts (armhole edge), k to last 5 sts, M1 (collar inc), k5. Knit next row. Cont to shape armhole as

SIZES

Instructions are written for size Small. Changes for Medium, Large, and X-Large are in parentheses.

KNITTED MEASUREMENTS

- **Bust (closed) 37 (39, 43, 46)"/94 (99, 109, 117)cm**
- **Length 24½ (25, 25½, 26)"/62 (63.5, 64.5, 66)cm**
- **Upper arm 13½ (14½, 15½, 16½)"/34 (37, 39.5, 42)cm**

MATERIALS

- **8 (8, 9, 10) balls in #112 red of *Wool-Ease Chunky* by Lion Brand, 5oz/140g balls, each approx 153yd/140m (acrylic/wool)**
- **One pair size 10½ (6.5mm) needles or size to obtain gauge**
- **One size 10½ (6.5mm) needle for three-needle bind off**
- **Stitch holders**

GAUGE

12 sts and 24 rows to 4"/10cm over garter st using size 10½ (6.5mm) needles.

Take time to check gauge.

foll: dec 1 st at armhole edge on next row, then every other row 1 (2, 3, 3) times more. AT THE SAME TIME, inc 1 st (M1) 5 sts from collar edge every 4th row 5 times more, then every 6th row twice—33 (34, 35, 37) sts. Work even until armhole measures same as back to shoulder, end with a WS row.

Shoulder shaping

Bind off 4 (5, 5, 6) sts at armhole edge twice, then 5 (4, 5, 5) sts once—20 sts. Work even for 3"/7.5cm for collar, end with a WS row. Place sts on holder.

RIGHT FRONT

Work as for left front, reversing all shaping.

SLEEVES

Cast on 27 (27, 29, 29) sts. Cont in garter st and work even for 6 rows. Inc 1 st each side on next row, then every 14th (12th, 10th, 8th) row 6 (7, 8, 9) times more—41 (43, 47, 49) sts. Work even until piece measures 17½"/44.5cm from beg, end with a WS row.

Cap shaping

Bind off 3 (3, 4, 4) sts at beg of next 2 rows. Dec 1 st each side on next row, then every other row twice more, every 4th row 5 (6, 6, 7) times, every row 4 (4, 5, 5) times. Bind off rem 11 sts.

FINISHING

Do not block. Sew shoulder seams.

Three-needle bind-off

To bind off and join collar sts tog, work as foll: Place sts on holders on two separate needles. Hold needles parallel with RS facing and tips of needles pointing right. Insert 3rd needle knitwise into first st on front needle and first st on back needle, then wrap the yarn around the 3rd needle as if to knit. Knit these 2 sts tog and slip them off the needles. *Knit the next 2 sts tog in the same manner. Slip the first st on the 3rd needle over the 2nd st and off the needle. Rep from * across the row until all sts have been bound off. Sew inside collar edge to back neck edge. Set in sleeves. Sew side and sleeve seams.

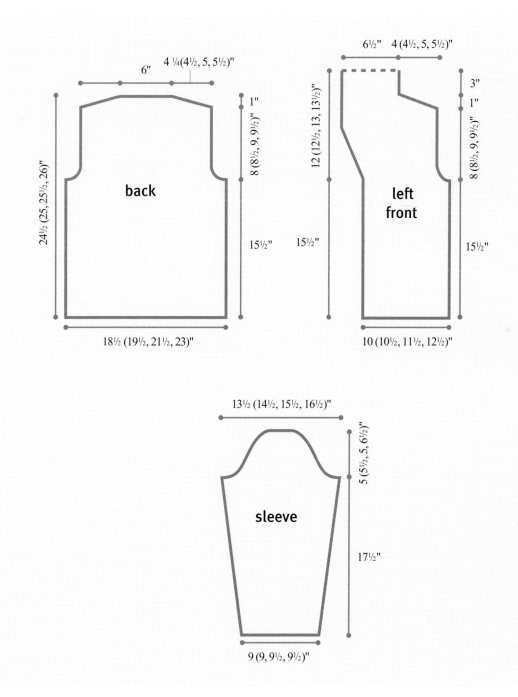

SIZES

Instructions are written for size 1–2 months. Changes for sizes 3–6 months, 9–12 months, and 18–24 months are in parentheses.

KNITTED MEASUREMENTS

- **Chest (closed) 21 (23½, 25, 28)"/53.5 (59.5, 63.5, 71)cm**
- **Length 8½ (9½, 10½, 12½)"/21.5 (24, 26.5, 31.5)cm**
- **Upper arm 8 (10, 11½, 13)"/20.5 (25.5, 29, 33)cm**

MATERIALS

- **3 (4, 5, 7) balls in #98 cream (MC) and 1 ball in #110 navy (CC) of _Cashmere Blend_ by Lion Brand, 1½oz/40g balls, each approx 84yd/71m (wool, nylon, cashmere)**
- **One pair size 8 (5mm) needles or size to obtain gauge**
- **Size G/6 (4mm) crochet hook**

GAUGE

17 sts and 24 rows to 4"/10cm over St st using size 8 (5mm) needles.
Take time to check gauge.

Baby sweater

Who can resist spoiling a new baby? Whether it's your own grandchild or somebody else's bundle of joy, greet the new arrival with this cashmere blend sweater by Veronica Manno. Contrasting crochet trim completes the look.

BACK

With MC, cast on 46 (50, 54, 60) sts. Work even in St st until piece measures 8½ (9½, 10½, 12½)"/21.5 (24, 26.5, 31.5)cm from beg, end with a WS row. Bind off.

LEFT FRONT

With MC, cast on 26 (28, 30, 33) sts. Work even in St st until piece measures 7 (8, 9, 11)"/17.5 (20.5, 23, 28)cm from beg, end with a RS row.

Neck shaping

Next row (WS) Bind off 5 sts, work to end. Cont to bind off 3 sts from neck edge twice, then 2 sts once—13 (15, 17, 20) sts. Work even until piece measures same length as back to shoulder.

RIGHT FRONT

Work as for left front, reversing neck shaping.

SLEEVES

With MC, cast on 26 (28, 30, 32) sts. Cont in St st for 6 rows. Inc 1 st each side on next row, then every 8th (4th, 4th, 4th) row 3 (1, 5, 9) times more, every 0 (6th, 6th, 6th) rows 0 (5, 3, 2) times—34 (42, 48, 56) sts. Work even until piece measures 6 (7½, 8½, 10)"/15 (19, 21.5, 25.5)cm from beg, end with a WS row. Bind off.

FINISHING

Lightly block pieces to measurements. Sew shoulder seams. Place markers at 4 (5, 5¾, 6½)"/10 (12.5, 14.5, 16.5)cm down from shoulders on fronts and back. Sew sleeves between markers. Sew side and sleeve seams.

Edging

From RS, with crochet hook, join CC with a sl st in left side seam. **Rnd 1** Ch 1, making sure that work lies flat, sc evenly around entire outer edge, working 2 sc in each corner. Join rnd with a sl st in first sc. Fasten off.

Sleeve edging

From RS, with crochet hook, join CC with a sl st in underarm seam. **Rnd 1** Ch 1, sc in each st around. Join rnd with a sl st in first sc. Fasten off.

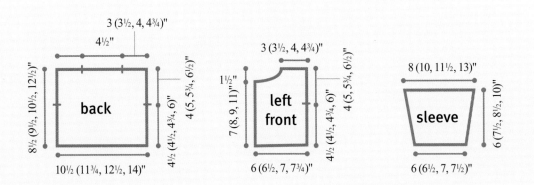

Fuzzy mittens

These mittens will be a real conversation starter. Knit them—on five needles!—in a bright color of this nubby, textured yarn. Designed by Veronica Manno.

MATERIALS

• **1 ball in #112 rose (MC) of** *Lion Bouclé* **by Lion Brand,** 2½oz/70g balls, each approx 57yd/52m (acrylic/mohair/nylon)
• **1 ball in #140 rose (CC) of** *Lion Wool* **by Lion Brand,** 3oz/85g balls, each approx 158yd/144m (wool)
• **One set (5) size 8 (5mm) dpn or size to obtain gauge**
• **Stitch marker**
• **Stitch holder**

GAUGE

12 sts to 4"/10cm over St st using MC and size 8 (5mm) dpn. Take time to check gauge.

Fuzzy mittens

LEFT MITTEN

With CC, cast 10 sts onto first dpn, 10 sts onto 2nd dpn, 10 sts onto 3rd dpn, and 10 sts onto 4th dpn—40 sts. Join and place marker to indicate beg of rnds. Work around in k1, p1 rib for 3"/7.5cm. Next rnd knit, dec 16 sts evenly spaced—24 sts. Change to MC.

Thumb gusset

Rnd 1 K9, M1, k2, M1, k13—26 sts.

Rnds 2 and 3 Knit.

Rnd 4 K9, M1, k4, M1, k13—28 sts.

Rnds 5 and 6 Knit.

Rnd 7 K9, M1, k6, M1, k13—30 sts.

Rnds 8 and 9 Knit.

Next rnd K9, place next 8 sts on holder for thumb, k13.

Next rnd K9, cast on 2 sts, k13—24 sts.

Hand

Cont in St st until piece measures 9"/23cm from beg or length to top of index finger.

Top shaping

Rnd 1 K1, SKP, k6, k2tog, k2, SKP, k6, k2tog, k1—20 sts.

Rnd 2 K1, SKP, k4, k2tog, k2, SKP, k4, k2tog, k1—16 sts.

Rnd 3 K1, SKP, k2, k2tog, k2, SKP, k2, k2tog, k1—12 sts.

Rnd 4 K1, SKP, k2tog, k2, SKP, k2tog, k1—8 sts. Cut yarn leaving a long tail. Thread tail in tapestry needle and weave through sts. Pull tight to gather, fasten off securely.

Thumb

With CC, k first 4 sts from holder with first dpn, k rem 4 sts from

holder with 2nd dpn, pick up and k 2 sts in first cast-on st of hand with 3rd dpn, then pick up and k 2 sts in 2nd cast-on st of hand with 4th dpn—12 sts. Cont in St st for 1¼"/3cm or 3 rows less than length to top of thumb.

Next rnd [K2tog, k1] 4 times—8 sts.

Next rnd [K2tog] 4 times—4 sts.

Last rnd [K2tog] twice—2 sts. Cut yarn leaving a long end. Thread tail in tapestry needle and weave through sts. Pull tight to gather, fasten off securely.

RIGHT MITTEN

Work as for left mitten to thumb gusset.

Thumb gusset

Rnd 1 K13, M1, k2, M1, k9—26 sts.

Rnds 2 and 3 Knit.

Rnd 4 K13, M1, k4, M1, k9—28 sts.

Rnds 5 and 6 Knit.

Rnd 7 K13, M1, k6, M1, k9—30 sts.

Rnds 8 and 9 Knit.

Next rnd K13, place next 8 sts on holder for thumb, k9.

Next rnd K13, cast on 2 sts, k9—24 sts. Cont to work as for left mitten.

Shawl Collar pullover

Make this one for your hubby, your son—or yourself! Designed by Pauline Schultz, this shawl-collared beauty adds interest for the knitter and the wearer with multiple ribbing patterns and rich colors.

PATTERN STITCH

(multiple of 6 sts)

Row 1 (RS) With B, *p3, k3; rep from * to end.

Row 2 With B, *k3, p3; rep from * to end.

Row 3 With A, rep row 1.

Row 4 With A, rep row 2.

Rep rows 1–4 for pat st.

K3, P3 RIB

(multiple of 6 sts plus 3)

Row 1 (RS) K3, *p3, k3; rep from * to end.

Row 2 P3, *k3, p3; rep from * to end.

Rep rows 1 and 2 for k3, p3 rib.

K1, P1 RIB

(multiple of 2 sts plus 1)

Row 1 (RS) K1, *p1, k1; rep from * to end.

Row 2 P1, *k1, p1; rep from * to end.

Rep rows 1 and 2 for k1, p1 rib.

SIZES

Instructions are written for men's size Small, Medium, Large, and X-Large are in parentheses.

KNITTED MEASUREMENTS

• Chest 40 (44, 48, 52)"/101.5 (111.5, 122, 132)cm

• Length 25 (25½, 26½, 27½)"/63.5 (64.5, 67.5, 70)cm

• Upper arm 18 (19, 20, 21)"/45.5 (48, 51, 53.5)cm

MATERIALS

• 4 (5, 5, 6) balls in #152 charcoal (A) and 3 (3, 3, 4) balls in #135 spice (B) of *Wool-Ease Chunky* by Lion Brand, 5oz/140g balls, each approx 153yd/140m (acrylic/wool)

• One pair each sizes 8 and 10½ (5 and 6.5mm) needles or size to obtain gauge

• Size 8 (5mm) circular needle, 36"/91.5cm long

GAUGE

12 sts and 24 rows to 4"/10cm over pat st using larger needles. Take time to check gauge.

BACK

With smaller needles and A, cast on 57 (63, 69, 75) sts. Work in k3, p3 rib for 2½"/6.5cm, inc 3 sts evenly spaced across last row and end with a WS row—60 (66, 72, 78) sts. Change to larger needles and cont in pat st until piece measures 15½ (15½, 16, 16½)"/39.5 (39.5, 40.5, 42) cm from beg, end with a WS row.

Armhole shaping

Bind off 4 (4, 5, 6) sts at beg of next 2 rows. Dec 1 st each side every other row 4 (5, 5, 6) times—44 (48, 52, 54) sts. Work even until armhole measures 9 (9½, 10, 10½)"/23 (24, 25.5, 26.5), end with a WS row.

Neck and shoulder shaping

Next row (RS) Work across first 13 (15, 16, 17) sts, join another ball of yarn and bind off center 18 (18, 20, 20) sts for back neck, work to end. Working both sides at once, dec 1 st at each neck edge once. Bind off rem 12 (14, 15, 16) sts each side for shoulders.

FRONT

Work as for back until armhole shaping is completed, end with a WS row—
44 (48, 52, 54) sts.

Neck and shoulder shaping

Next row (RS) Work across first 15 (17, 18, 19) sts, join another ball of
yarn and bind off center 14 (14, 16, 16) sts for front neck, work to end.
Working both sides at once, work even for 2"/5cm. Dec 1 st at each neck
edge on next row, then every 12th row twice more. When piece measures
same length as back to shoulders, bind off rem 12 (14, 15, 16) sts each side
for shoulders.

SLEEVES

With smaller needles and A cast on 33 sts. Work in k3, p3 rib for
2½"/6.5cm, inc 3 sts evenly spaced across last row and end on WS—36 sts.

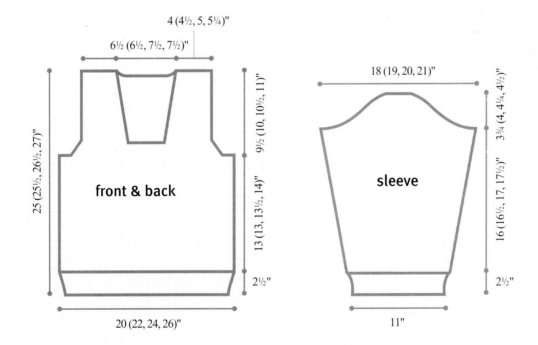

4 (4½, 5, 5¼)"

6½ (6½, 7½, 7½)"

9½ (10, 10½, 11)"

25 (25½, 26½, 27)"

front & back

13 (13, 13½, 14)"

2½"

20 (22, 24, 26)"

18 (19, 20, 21)"

3¾ (4, 4¼, 4½)"

sleeve

16 (16½, 17, 17½)"

2½"

11"

Change to larger needles. Cont in pat st and work even for 1"/2.5cm, end with a WS row. Inc 1 st each side on next row, then every 10th (8th, 8th, 6th) row 8 (10, 11, 14) times more—54 (58, 60, 66) sts. Work even until piece measures 18½ (19, 19½, 20)"/47 (48, 49.5, 51) cm from beg, end with a WS row.

Cap shaping

Bind off 4 (4, 5, 6) sts at beg of next 2 rows. Dec 1 st each side on next row, then every row 4 (5, 5, 7) times more, every other row 7 times, bind off 5 sts at beg of next 2 rows. Bind off rem 12 (14, 14, 14) sts.

FINISHING

Block pieces to measurements. Sew shoulder seams.

Collar

With RS facing, circular needle and A, pick up and k 37 (37, 39, 39) sts along right neck edge to shoulder seam, 21 (21, 23, 23) sts along back neck edge to shoulder seam, then 37 (37, 39, 39) sts along left neck edge—95 (95, 101, 101) sts. Beg with row 2 (WS), work even in k1, p1 rib for 4½ (4½, 5½, 5½)"/11.5 (11.5, 14, 14) cm. Bind off loosely in rib. Set in sleeves. Sew side and sleeve seams. Sew down side edges of collar at center front, over-lapping left side over right side.

Garter Ridge socks

Knitting with 5 needles may feel awkward at first, but once you've gotten the hang of it, knitting socks can be addictive. Judy Sumner's design features a patterned cuff, short row heel, and self-patterning yarn to keep you interested from top to toe.

SIZES

One size fits women's shoe size 7–8 (39/40).

KNITTED MEASUREMENTS

Leg circumference 7"/17.5cm

Foot length 9"/23cm

MATERIALS

• 1 ball in #207 regatta blue stripe of *Magic Stripes* by Lion Brand, 3½oz/100g balls, each approx 330yd/300m (wool/nylon)

• One set (5) size 2 (2.5mm) dpn or size to obtain gauge

• Stitch marker

GAUGE

28 sts and 36 rnds to 4"/10cm over St st using size 2 (2.5mm) needles.

Take time to check gauge.

GARTER RIDGE PATTERN

(multiple of 6 sts)

Note Slip all sts as if to purl.

Rnds 1 and 2 Knit.

Rnd 3 *K4, slip 2 wyib; rep from * around.

Rnd 4 *P4, slip 2 wyib; rep from * around.

Rnds 5 and 6 Knit.

Rnd 7 K1, *slip 2 wyib, k4; rep from * to last 3 sts, k3.

Rnd 8 P1, *slip 2 wyib, p4; rep from * to last 3 sts, p3.

Rep rnds 1–8 for garter ridge pat.

SOCK

Beg at cuff edge, cast on 48 sts. Place 12 sts on each of 4 needles. Join, taking care not to twist sts on needles and place marker to indicate beg of rnd. Work around in k1, p1 rib for 1½"/4cm. Cont in garter ridge pat and work until leg measures approx 6"/15cm from beg, end with rnd 1 or 5.

Heel flap

Knit 12 (needle #1), dropping marker. Turn work. You will now be working back and forth in St st as follows:

Row 1 (WS) Slip 1, p 23 (needles #1 and #4). Place these sts onto one needle for heel flap; leave rem sts on needles #2 and #3 unworked.

Row 2 *Slip 1, k1; rep from * to end.

Row 3 Slip 1, p to end.

Rep rows 2 and 3 until 23 rows have been completed, end with row 3.
Turn heel.

Row 1 (RS) Slip 1, k13, SKP, k1. Turn.

Row 2 Slip 1, p5, p2tog, p1. Turn.

Row 3 Slip 1, k6, SKP, k1. Turn.

Row 4 Slip 1, p7, p2tog, p1. Turn. Cont in this manner, working one more stitch before the dec on each row until 14 sts rem.

Gussets

Knit across 14 heel sts, then pick up and k 12 sts along side edge of heel flap, M1 between heel flap and needle #2; knit across needles #2 and #3; M1 between needle #3 and heel flap, pick up and k 12 sts along opposite side edge of heel flap; k 7. Place marker to indicate beg of rnd and center of heel. Cont to work in the round in St st as foll:

Shape instep

Next rnd Knit around, knitting each M1 st tog with gusset st next to it on each side.

Dec rnd K to last 3 sts on needle #1, end SKP, k1; knit sts on needles #2 and #3 (instep sts); for needle #4, k1, k2tog, k to end of rnd.

Next rnd Rep last 2 rnds until there are 12 sts on each needle—48 sts.

Foot

Work even until foot measures approx 7½"/19cm from back of heel or 1½"/4cm less than desired length .

Shape toe

Dec rnd *K to 3 sts from end of needle, k2tog, k1; k1, SKP, k to end of needle; rep from * once more.

Next rnd Knit. Rep last 2 rnds until 5 sts remain on each needle—20 sts. Combine sts on needles #1 and #4 onto one needle and sts on needles #2 and #3 onto another needle.

Graft toe

Thread a blunt tapestry needle with one of the yarn ends. Hold the 2 needles parallel with WS sides tog. Insert tapestry needle as if to purl into first stitch on front needle, then insert tapestry needle as if to knit into first stitch on back needle. Cont to work as foll:

1 Insert tapestry needle as if to knit through first st on front needle and let st drop from needle.

2 Insert tapestry needle into 2nd st on front needle as if to purl and pull yarn through, leaving st on needle.

3 Insert tapestry needle into first st on back needle as if to purl and let st drop from needle.

4 Insert tapestry needle as if to knit through 2nd st on back needle and pull the yarn through, leaving st on needle. Rep steps 1–4 until all sts are grafted tog. If necessary, adjust tension of grafting yarn to make sts even across. Weave in ends.

Notes

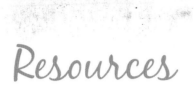

Resources

Lion Brand Yarn Co.
34 West 15th Street
New York, NY 10011
Visit Lion Brand's website for more than 1000 knit and crochet patterns:
www.LionBrand.com